THE EASY COLLEGE COOKBOOK

the easy COLLEGE COOKBOOK

75 Quick, Affordable Recipes for Campus Life

CANDACE BRAUN DAVISON

PHOTOGRAPHY BY PAUL SIRISALEE

ROCKRIDGE PRESS

For general information on our other products and services or to obtain technical support, please contact our Customer Care Department within the United States at (866) 744-2665, or outside the United States at (510) 253-0500.

Rockridge Press publishes its books in a variety of electronic and print formats. Some content that appears in print may not be available in electronic books, and vice versa.

Interior and Cover Designer: Linda Snorina

Art Producer: Hillary Frileck

Editor: Crystal Nero

Production Manager: Oriana Siska

Production Editor: Melissa Edeburn

Photography © 2019 Paul Sirisalee

Food styling by Caitlin Haught Brown

Author photo courtesy of © Nathan Davison

ISBN: Print 978-1-64152-938-9
eBook 978-1-64152-939-6

R0

**To Nathan and Emerie,
a.k.a. the best arouuuund!**

Contents

CHAPTER 5: SIMPLE SALADS 59

CHAPTER 6: SUPER SOUPS 71

CHAPTER 7: RICE, NOODLES, AND PASTA 85

CHAPTER 8: HEARTY MAINS 107

CHAPTER 9: DESSERTS 129

Creamery
Butter
NET WT. 4 OZ.

Introduction

Don't let all those competition shows on TV intimidate you—cooking is honestly as simple as combining ingredients to create something that tastes incredible. Every recipe in this book has been simplified to its most basic components, with guidance on exactly what to look for so you know when your meal's cooked to perfection. There's no need to stress, even if the most impressive dish you've ever made are well-done (okay, borderline burned) Pop-Tarts®. Although this book won't teach you how to run a Michelin-starred restaurant out of your dorm room (there are food safety laws against that), you will learn how to eat well—quickly, easily, and on a budget. So don't worry about having chef-caliber knife skills or knowing French culinary terms; bring your appetite, and this book will take care of the rest.

GREEK FLATBREAD
(PAGE 108)

chapter 1

INTRO TO COOKING

Before you dive into these recipes, you'll want to stock your pantry. Here you'll find ideas for creating a makeshift one in your dorm room, along with tips for investing in appliances to make every recipe in this book. You'll even learn some tricks that will inspire you to whip up your own creations.

Why Cook?

Even if you're staying in a state-of-the-art dorm with your own kitchen and a robot butler (that's a thing, right?), finding time to cook can be a pain. I get it. There's a dining hall just down the street that's perpetually serving your go-to guilty pleasures—pizza, chicken tenders, troughs of French fries. And don't get me started on the soft-serve machine. The temptation is *great*. And so is the cost. Hitting up the caf for every meal didn't make financial sense for me, especially when I factored in the need to shop for new jeans in a bigger size. (Curse you, soft-serve machine!)

So, I started cooking. At first I made simple breakfasts and snacks, like the ones in the opening chapters of this cookbook. You can also ease into cooking, beginning with meals that cost just a few dollars to make—and that take just as much time to whip up as you'd spend waiting in line at the dining hall or the drive-thru.

The dishes in these pages call for whole foods rather than processed ingredients, but that doesn't mean *every recipe* in this book is healthy. The goal is healthy-ish, because sometimes you need to celebrate, and what's better than a freshly baked cookie?! Or cake in a mug! The bottom line: Cooking should be fun. Every recipe here is designed to make you look forward to getting into the kitchen. Or that microwave-topped shelf you've generously dubbed a "kitchenette."

As Easy as It Gets

The recipes in this book have been designed to avoid the need for a ton of kitchen gadgets and pricey ingredients. If you have a skillet, saucepan, mixing bowl, chef's knife, toaster oven, microwave, and hot plate or access to a stovetop, you can make just about E-V-E-R-Y-T-H-I-N-G included in these pages. Some recipes require only one bowl because

1. Who has space for a ton of bowls?
2. Who has the time (or desire) to do dishes?
3. Doesn't food taste better when there's hardly any cleanup?

If you're immediately protesting that your dorm won't allow a toaster oven or hot plate, I hear you. A hot plate is really just one burner on a stovetop, so for those recipes calling for one, you can use your residence hall's communal kitchen. And because I know all too well what it's like to be halfway through dinner and see three other people hovering around me, waiting to use the oven, I've made these recipes not only easy but fast.

Every recipe clearly identifies the main appliance it uses, the time it takes to make, and any cooking requirements (spoiler: Many recipes don't have one!). Some also address special dietary needs. Maybe you're vegan, trying out Meatless Mondays, or your roommate doesn't do gluten or is allergic to nuts. Throughout the cookbook, you'll find tips on easy substitutions to make a dish fit your lifestyle.

MONEY HACKS

Shop for small appliances in September. That's when many stores roll out new models, offering steep discounts on last year's microwaves.

Look before you shop. Don't add anything to a cart without first searching for a promo code.

Double-check the cost per ounce before buying in bulk. It's typically listed on the left side of the price tag on store shelves. Use this information to compare prices more easily. Bulk isn't always the cheapest option.

Shop big box stores for nonperishables. Canned vegetables, flour, sugar, oil, and other essentials are often cheaper in stores such as Target, Walmart, or major grocery chains.

Split the cost of seasonings and condiments with your roommate. This strategy is one of the best ways to keep your grocery bill from adding up. You'll probably use only one bottle of something like oregano for the whole year. (However, if one of you is a sriracha addict, it may be better for each of you to buy your own so you can avoid "You used it all—AGAIN?!" arguments.)

The Secrets of Great Flavor

Recipes, like rules, are meant to be broken. Consider them to be general guidelines so you get reliable results. The key is to think about your ideal bite and what you might need to tweak in the recipe to suit your tastes. If you make something and it's a little bland for your liking, consider adjusting one of the four essential elements of cooking: salt, fat, acid, heat. They're not just the title of a Netflix show and *New York Times*-bestselling cookbook. As chef and writer Samin Nosrat revealed, adjusting a dish's salt or acidity (for example, by adding a little lemon juice or vinegar) can intensify flavor. A little fat can give a dish a silkier, smoother texture and keep meat or vegetables from sticking to the pan. Knowing when to turn up the heat—and when to turn it off—can mean the difference between a gray, rubbery steak and one you'd gladly splurge on at a steakhouse.

Cooking is all about tasting as you go, making adjustments, and keeping an eye out for signs of doneness. Tasting as you go may be even more important than following strict measurements and exact timing because the more you practice, the better you'll get. I promise.

Get Your Kitchen(ette) in Order

No matter how cramped your space is, you can put together a workstation that lets you create all kinds of meals—without having to leave the comfort of your 9-by-9 foot room.

ESSENTIAL TOOLS AND EQUIPMENT

Thankfully, you don't need a lot of tools to master the basics, even if a casual stroll of the kitchen section of any store would suggest otherwise. (What? You don't have a separate corer, slicer, and masher to make your avocado toast?! The horror!) Here's all you really need to make some great grub.

Tools

CAN OPENER: There are plenty of hacks online showing you how to use a knife to open a can. Ignore them. Yes, it can be done, but it's so easy to slip and cut your hand that you're better off spending a few bucks on the real deal.

CASSEROLE DISH: A standard 2-quart oven-safe casserole dish should fit in an average toaster oven. This dish or a 9-by-5 inch loaf pan will handle many of the main courses in this book.

KNIVES: An 8-inch chef's knife, a paring knife, and a butter knife are all you need to whip up just about anything in this book.

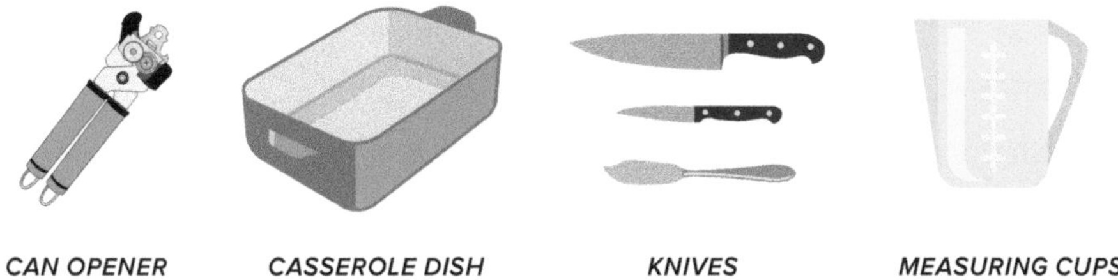

CAN OPENER *CASSEROLE DISH* *KNIVES* *MEASURING CUPS*

MEASURING CUPS AND SPOONS: All you need is one liquid measuring cup and a set of dry measuring cups, along with a basic set of measuring spoons, to get a consistently good meal every time. Your half-cup measuring cup can double as a ladle.

MIXING BOWL: One medium 3- or 4-quart bowl will be big enough to stir just about anything without ingredients splashing out. Bonus if it's microwave safe.

OVEN MITTS: If you don't have easy access to the laundry, go for a silicone pair—they are easy to rinse and wipe clean.

RESEALABLE PLASTIC BAGS: The gallon-size bags are great for marinating chicken and other meats.

SAUCEPAN: Look for a 3- to 4-quart size. It's perfect to cook just about anything. (A saucepot's just as good. It has two small hook-like handles, whereas a saucepan has one long handle.)

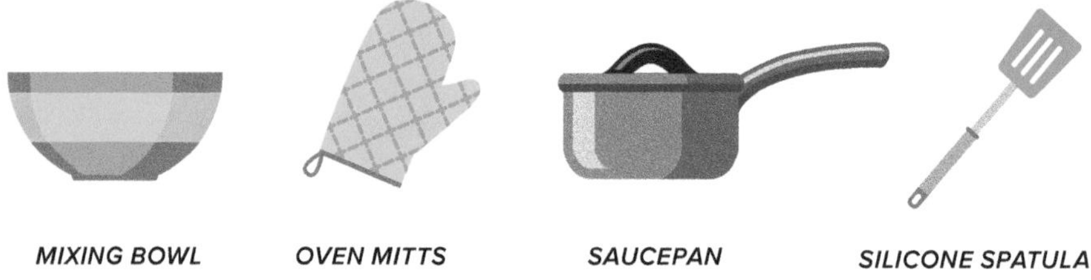

SILICONE SPATULA: This tool is a must for getting every last drop of batter out of a bowl.

SKILLET: Spring for a 12-inch pan and you can make any recipe in this book without worrying about crowding (or accidentally sending ingredients flying as you attempt to stir or flip them). For beginner cooks, I recommend a nonstick pan so you don't have to worry about seasoning the pan to prevent food from sticking, as you would with cast iron, for example.

TONGS: Flip veggies or meat easily with a pair of tongs.

VEGETABLE PEELER: This tool can double as a sort of spiralizer. Just keep peeling and—voilà!—you've created ribbons of delicious faux pasta.

Equipment

BLENDER: A mini blender can be great for mixing smoothies to sip on the go, but you can also use it to purée soups and quickly chop vegetables—a few fast pulses and you're done.

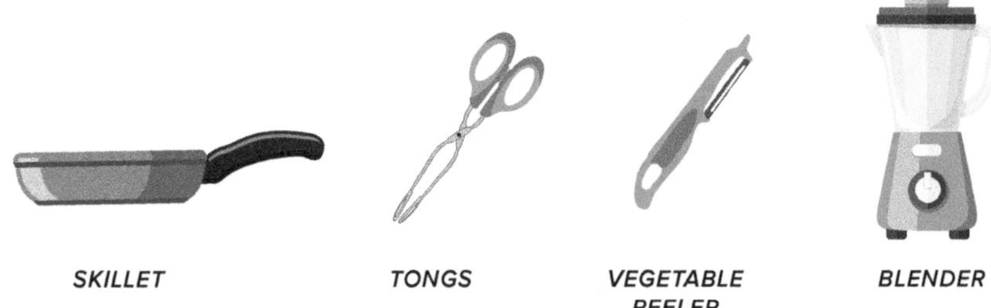

SKILLET *TONGS* *VEGETABLE PEELER* *BLENDER*

HAND MIXER: If you love to bake, you need a hand mixer. Sure, you can mix ingredients by hand with a spoon, but for ice creams and cake batters, you'll get the job done faster and with better results using an inexpensive electric hand mixer. If you bake less than once a month, stick to the spoon or try shaking your ingredients in a lidded jar.

HOT PLATE/STOVETOP: These days, it's rare to find a residence hall that allows you to use a hot plate, which is essentially a burner on a stovetop. However, many schools offer access to a nearby communal kitchen.

MICROWAVE: Many dorms allow 1,000-watt microwave ovens, but some allow only 700-watt ovens, so check with your RA before hauling one to campus. All the recipes in this book are tested using a standard, 1,000-watt model. If yours is 700 watts, it'll take a little more time to cook each dish, and you may have to stop mid-cooking to stir the food to ensure there aren't cold spots. Every recipe will include visual cues to help you check for doneness.

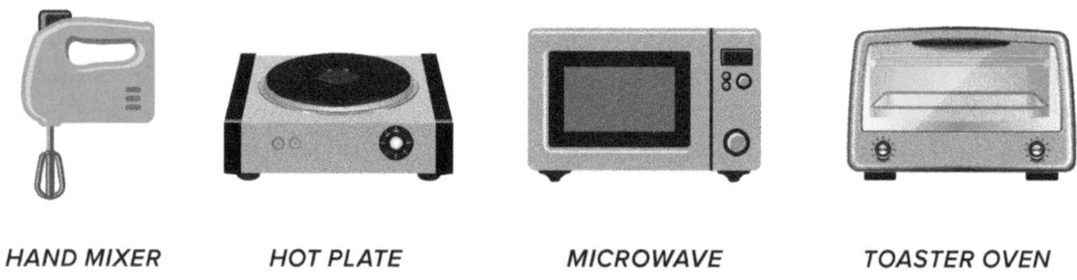

HAND MIXER *HOT PLATE* *MICROWAVE* *TOASTER OVEN*

MINI FRIDGE: Look for a model with a freezer to store frozen fruit for smoothies or to freeze no-churn ice cream. Most schools allow refrigerators that are 4 cubic feet or smaller; check with your school to be sure. Look for a fridge with ample depth. (Stow leftover meals in resealable plastic bags so you can fit more in your fridge at one time.)

TOASTER OVEN: Anything you can cook in an oven, you can whip up in a toaster oven—in smaller quantities. Because the heating elements in toaster ovens can vary, always check your meal for signs of doneness 5 minutes before the stated cooking time.

APPLIANCE HACK

Wait—You Can Do That with a Microwave?

If you're only using the microwave oven to reheat leftovers and warm canned soup, you're missing out on creative opportunities. With these tips, you can make microwave meals taste practically gourmet.

Zap citrus in the microwave for 10 seconds. The heat softens the fruit and makes it easier to squeeze, so you can get more juice from it.

Create a well in the middle of dense meals, like tamale pie or pastas. Microwaves heat food from the outside in, so this technique will help the food cook more evenly.

Let baked goods sit for a minute before digging in. Sometimes, a mug muffin or cake won't look fully cooked, but once it sits for 60 seconds, it'll firm up.

Place a cup of water next to your food in the microwave. The steam will keep the meal from drying out.

Wrap sandwiches, tortillas, and bread in a damp paper towel before heating them. That way they won't harden.

FRIDGE AND PANTRY

Your space is limited, which means you need to make use of every square inch you have, and you don't want to waste it with condiments you'll rarely use. Here is a list of ingredients worth keeping on hand, along with ideas for stashing them.

For the Mini Fridge

BUTTER: Choose unsalted butter; you can always add salt to your dish later.

CONDIMENTS: Stock up on the basics at the drive-thru or when you get takeout, such as ketchup, mustard, mayo, barbecue sauce, and soy sauce. Store extra condiment packets in a resealable bag in your fridge. You never know when they'll come in handy, and will take up far less mini-fridge space than a bunch of bulky bottles.

EGGS: Size matters. The recipes here call for large eggs, and you can buy them by the half dozen so they won't take up too much space in the fridge.

MILK: All recipes in this book were tested using 2 percent milk, though some people prefer whole milk because it can add a creamier consistency to recipes—go with what you're most likely to use.

SCALLIONS: Want the flavor of an onion without tearing up as you slice—or trying to figure out what the heck to do with the rest of the bulb? Buy a bunch of scallions. Also sold as green onions, the white part has a stronger flavor, like a white onion, whereas the green part is more mellow.

SHREDDED CHEESE: This cheese, which comes pre-shredded at most grocery stores, is the key to taking any dish to the next level. Most recipes call for sharp Cheddar cheese or Mexican-style cheese blend, but feel free to use your favorite cheese.

For the Makeshift Pantry

FLOUR: Buy all-purpose flour, which is what the recipes in this book call for. You can use bleached or unbleached.

GARLIC POWDER: If you don't have space in the mini fridge for a jar of minced garlic (or the patience to mince fresh garlic), get the powder.

HOT SAUCE: Whether you're into sriracha, Cholula, or some small-batch need-to-sign-a-waiver-before-buying Carolina Reaper nonsense, hot sauce will give your food a kick.

OLIVE OIL: This oil is great for sautéing dishes and dressing salads and pastas.

SALT AND PEPPER: Season throughout the cooking process with these two staples.

SUGAR: Store sugar in a resealable plastic bag or an airtight container to keep out ants (and humidity).

MINI-MART SHOPPING LIST

No grocery store nearby? No problem. Stock up on these essentials at your nearest convenience store:

CANNED AND BOTTLED ITEMS

- Beans
- Marinara sauce
- Vegetables
- Water

DAIRY AND EGGS

- Eggs, large
- Greek yogurt
- Shredded cheese
- String cheese
- Unsalted butter

MEAT

- Bacon
- Cold cuts
- Hot dogs

PANTRY ITEMS

- All-purpose flour
- Bread
- Instant ramen
- Microwave popcorn
- Oil (canola, olive, or vegetable)
- Pasta
- Pepper
- Salt
- Vinegar

PRODUCE

- Apples
- Bananas
- Baby carrots
- Celery (often found in grab-and-go snack packs)
- Cherry tomatoes
- Cucumbers
- Lemons
- Limes
- Mango
- Pineapple chunks
- Strawberries
- Watermelon chunks (look for fruit cups)

Common Cooking Terms

AL DENTE: Cooking pasta until tender yet still firm.

BEAT: Mixing ingredients so fast that you're stirring air into them, resulting in a lighter, fluffier texture. You can mix by hand but using an electric hand mixer is faster.

BOIL: Heating water over high heat until it bubbles vigorously. You'll know you've reached a boil when the bubbles are large, cover the entire surface of the liquid, and emit some steam.

CHOP: Cutting an ingredient into ½-inch to 1-inch bite-size pieces.

DICE: Cutting an ingredient into ⅛-inch to ¼-inch pieces.

DREDGE: Dipping meat or vegetables into a wet mixture such as whisked eggs or milk and then into a dry mixture such as bread crumbs before cooking.

FOLD: Gently mixing a delicate ingredient (like berries, which could burst) into a batter or dough using a rubber spatula.

MARINATE: Soaking an ingredient (like steak or chicken) in a liquid to tenderize it and infuse it with flavor.

MINCE: Cutting an ingredient to less than half the size of a dice to allow the ingredient to flavor a dish without changing its texture. Herbs and garlic are often minced.

SAUTÉ: Cooking an ingredient quickly over medium-high or high heat in a little oil or butter. Often, the ingredient will "jump" or sizzle when it hits the hot pan. The term *sauté* originates from the French infinitive "to jump."

SEAR: Quickly cooking large pieces of meat like steak or a roast over high heat to create a crisp exterior crust and retain a tender interior.

SIMMER: Heating a liquid to the point at which small bubbles form around the perimeter of the pan. This slow boil is maintained over medium heat.

STORAGE HACKS

Just because you don't have a designated kitchen area doesn't mean you can't create one. Here are a few storage hacks that will help you make the most of your space.

Buy a rolling utility cart. Get one with three trays, so you can store nonperishables on one level, dishes and utensils on another level, and your microwave and anything you tend to use all the time, like salt and pepper or a paper towel holder, on the top.

Repurpose an over-the-door shoe organizer. It's just the right size for storing nonperishable condiments, canned foods, measuring cups, dish towels, oven mitts, and utensils like tongs and spatulas.

Give that plastic, three-drawer organizer new life. Typically used to corral clothes or papers, they're even more useful holding your kitchenware and nonperishable food. Because they're plastic, they're easy to wipe clean of inevitable spills.

BREAKFAST TACOS
(PAGE 21)

chapter 2

BREAKFAST IN A FLASH

Microwave Bacon and Eggs

MICROWAVE

5-INGREDIENT

15 MINUTES OR LESS

Serves 1

PREP TIME
5 minutes

COOK TIME
3 minutes

Technique Tip: A cooking time of 1 minute per bacon slice is a good rule of thumb to follow, so if you're cooking 5 slices at once, microwave for 5 minutes.

Scrambled eggs and bacon seems like the kind of meal you reserve for the weekend—but it doesn't have to be. You can make the entire meal in the microwave in roughly as much time and with as much effort as you'd put into toasting and buttering bread. This technique's a game changer.

1 bacon slice, halved widthwise
2 large eggs
2 tablespoons milk
Salt
Pepper

1. Place the bacon halves on a microwave-safe plate lined with paper towels, keeping them just far enough apart that they aren't touching. Microwave for 45 seconds, check for doneness, and continue to microwave in 20-second intervals until you've reached your desired crispness.
2. Crack the eggs into a mug, add the milk, and whisk with a fork until the mixture is pale yellow. Season with salt and pepper. Microwave for 40 seconds. Stir and microwave 20 to 30 seconds more, or until the eggs are no longer runny.

PER SERVING: Calories: 263; Total fat: 20g; Carbohydrates: 2g; Fiber: 0g; Protein: 18g

Breakfast Tacos

In my opinion, there's nothing salsa and shredded cheese can't fix. You can make this meal in less than 10 minutes, so you won't miss that 8 a.m. class you stayed up all night cramming for.

MICROWAVE

15 MINUTES OR LESS

Serves 1

PREP TIME
5 minutes

COOK TIME
3 minutes

2 bacon slices, halved widthwise
2 large eggs
2 tablespoons milk
Salt
Pepper
2 corn tortillas
½ avocado, pitted and diced
1½ tablespoons shredded Mexican-style cheese blend
Fresh salsa, for topping

1. Place the bacon halves on a microwave-safe plate lined with paper towels, keeping them just far enough apart that they aren't touching. Microwave for 1 minute, check for doneness, and continue to microwave in 20-second intervals until you've reached your desired crispness. Let cool and crumble the bacon into bite-size pieces.
2. Crack the eggs into a mug, add the milk, and whisk with a fork until the mixture is pale yellow. Season with salt and pepper. Microwave for 40 seconds. Stir and microwave for 20 to 30 seconds more, or until the eggs are no longer runny.
3. Spoon the eggs equally on the tortillas. Top with the bacon, avocado, cheese, and salsa.

Preparation Tip: Got an extra few seconds? Wrap the tortillas in a damp paper towel and microwave them for 15 seconds. They're softer that way.

PER SERVING: Calories: 253; Total fat: 16g; Carbohydrates: 14g; Fiber: 3g; Protein: 13g

Potato Tot Frittata

MICROWAVE

15 MINUTES OR LESS

Serves 1

PREP TIME
5 minutes

COOK TIME
4 minutes

Preparation Tip: Let the tots thaw before microwaving them so they'll cook faster. Make sure to check the eggs after the first 1½ minutes and stir so you don't wind up with overcooked eggs in one part of the mug and cold, semi-frozen tots in another.

Tots are basically hash browns. By tossing a few into a frittata, you're creating a full breakfast in one bowl. It doesn't get any easier than this.

¼ bell pepper, any color, diced
¼ teaspoon unsalted butter
1 bacon slice, divided
1 teaspoon shredded sharp Cheddar cheese, divided
3 to 4 frozen potato tots, thawed
1 large egg
1 teaspoon milk
Salt
Pepper

1. In a medium microwave-safe bowl, combine the bell pepper and butter. Microwave for 30 seconds to soften the pepper.
2. Place the bacon on a microwave-safe plate lined with paper towels. Microwave for 1 minute, let cool, and crumble.
3. Take a pinch of bacon from a slice and a pinch of cheese to top the frittata, and set aside.
4. Add the rest of the bacon and cheese to the bowl with the bell pepper. Add the tots, egg, milk, and a dash of salt and pepper, stirring with a fork to combine.
5. Microwave at 80 percent power for 1½ minutes. Stir, breaking up the egg. If the egg is still runny, microwave in 20-second intervals, stirring between each, until the egg is set. Top with the reserved bacon and cheese.

PER SERVING: Calories: 296; Total fat: 17g; Carbohydrates: 25g; Fiber: 3g; Protein: 12g

English Muffin Avocado Toast

Lemon juice will keep the avocado from browning and will add a citrusy kick to this meal. If you don't mind a little heat, sprinkle on some red pepper flakes.

TOASTER OVEN

15 MINUTES OR LESS

VEGAN

Serves 1

PREP TIME
5 minutes

COOK TIME
5 minutes

1 English muffin, split
½ avocado, pitted
¼ lemon
Salt
Pepper
Red pepper flakes, for seasoning (optional)

1. Toast the English muffin in the toaster oven until it's as golden brown (or charred) as you like it.
2. In a small bowl, mash the avocado with a spoon until it's spreadable.
3. Spread the mashed avocado onto the toasted muffin halves. Drizzle with lemon juice and sprinkle with salt, pepper, and red pepper flakes (if using) to suit your taste.

MAKE IT GLUTEN FREE: Choose gluten-free English muffins (like Udi's® or Food for Life® brands) instead of traditional ones and always remember to check packaging ingredients to ensure foods, especially oats, were processed in a completely gluten-free facility.

PER SERVING: Calories: 224; Total fat: 10g; Carbohydrates: 30g; Fiber: 4g; Protein: 6g

Technique Tip: Mash the unused avocado half in a bowl and pour a thin layer of lemon juice over the top. Cover the bowl with plastic wrap that's touching the mashed avocado, which will keep it from browning. Use the leftover avocado in Guacamole for Two (page 35).

Toaster Oven Granola

TOASTER OVEN

30 MINUTES OR LESS

VEGAN

Serves 2

PREP TIME
5 minutes

COOK TIME
24 minutes

Substitution Tip: Allergic to nuts? Skip them entirely. Crushed pretzels or dried fruit also work great in this mix. (Similarly, if you're out of maple syrup, try honey but the granola won't be vegan.)

Warning: You may want to make a triple batch of this granola so you can have it later with milk or layered in a yogurt parfait. It's sweet and salty and chewy with a little crunch—and straight up addictive.

- **⅓ cup cashews**
- **1 cup rolled oats**
- **⅓ cup unsweetened coconut flakes**
- **3 tablespoons maple syrup**
- **2 tablespoons olive oil**
- **¼ cup dried cranberries**
- **⅛ teaspoon salt**

1. Preheat the toaster oven to 300°F.
2. Place the cashews in a resealable plastic bag. Seal the bag, and use a spoon or a book to break up the cashews into bite-size pieces. Transfer the cashew pieces to a medium bowl and add the oats, coconut flakes, maple syrup, olive oil, cranberries, and salt. Stir to combine.
3. Spread the mixture in an even layer on the toaster oven tray (you may need to bake this in two batches, depending on the size of your oven).
4. Bake for 22 to 24 minutes, or until the granola starts to brown. Let the granola cool until it hardens. Break up the cooled granola and store it in an airtight container. Serve with milk or yogurt and fresh fruit.

PER SERVING: Calories: 618; Total fat: 34g; Carbohydrates: 73g; Fiber: 8g; Protein: 10g

Peanut Butter and Strawberry Yogurt Parfaits

Some mornings you just want to treat yourself—without derailing your entire diet. This recipe looks and tastes decadent but it won't cause a sugar crash halfway through your first class of the day.

MICROWAVE

5-INGREDIENT

15 MINUTES OR LESS

VEGETARIAN

Serves 1

PREP TIME
5 minutes

COOK TIME
15 seconds

1 tablespoon creamy peanut butter

1 (5.3-ounce) cup strawberry Greek yogurt

5 or 6 fresh strawberries, stemmed and cut into slices

1 graham cracker, crumbled (optional)

1. Place the peanut butter in a small microwave-safe bowl and microwave for 15 seconds. Stir.
2. In a cup or a small bowl, layer half the yogurt, half the strawberries, half the peanut butter, and half the graham cracker crumbles (if using). Repeat. Eat immediately.

MAKE IT GLUTEN FREE: Trade the graham cracker for 1 tablespoon of rice-based cereal, like Nature's Path Whole O's™ or Rice Chex™, and always remember to check packaging ingredients to ensure foods, especially oats, were processed in a completely gluten-free facility.

PER SERVING: Calories: 313; Total fat: 10g; Carbohydrates: 40g; Fiber: 3g; Protein: 19g

Fun Fact:
Greek yogurt has roughly double the protein of regular nonfat yogurt, according to the USDA, which helps you feel full longer.

Brownie Batter Overnight Oats

NO COOK

5-INGREDIENT

VEGETARIAN

Serves 2

PREP TIME
5 minutes plus
1 hour chilling

Substitution Tip: For a healthier breakfast, substitute cacao nibs for the chocolate chips. They're rich in iron, fiber, magnesium, and antioxidants.

All that time you spent resisting the overwhelming urge to lick the bowl after baking a batch of brownies is about to pay off. These overnight oats have all the flavor of your favorite indulgence—minus the guilt. Bonus: The protein in the yogurt will keep you going all day.

1 cup steel cut oats

1 cup milk

1 (6-ounce) container vanilla Greek yogurt

1 (0.73-ounce) packet hot cocoa mix

1½ tablespoons mini semisweet chocolate chips

1. In a medium bowl, stir together the oats, milk, yogurt, and hot cocoa mix. Evenly divide the mixture between 2 cups or Mason jars. Cover with plastic wrap or lids and refrigerate for at least 1 hour, or overnight.
2. Just before serving, stir in the chocolate chips. Eat chilled.

PER SERVING: Calories: 224; Total fat: 4g; Carbohydrates: 26g; Fiber: 4g; Protein: 13g

Berry Pancakes in a Jar

If you're the type who meditates, works out, writes a paper, and cooks a full breakfast before your 8 a.m. class, I commend you. This recipe is for those of us who wake up 5 minutes before class starts and crave something hearty before racing across campus. You can whip up a batch and enjoy them throughout the week, no matter how time-strapped you are.

MICROWAVE

15 MINUTES OR LESS

VEGETARIAN

Serves 4

PREP TIME
10 minutes

COOK TIME
3 minutes

1 cup all-purpose flour
1 tablespoon baking powder
1 tablespoon sugar
1 teaspoon salt
1 cup milk
1 large egg
Mixed fresh or frozen berries, for topping
Maple syrup, for serving (optional)

1. In a medium bowl, stir together the flour, baking powder, sugar, and salt. Stir in the milk and egg, breaking up any large clumps in the batter, until combined.
2. Pour the batter into 4 microwave-safe mugs, filling them about one-fourth full.
3. Sprinkle some berries in each mug and add more batter on top, filling each half full.
4. Microwave the pancakes right away (see step 5), or cover the mugs with plastic wrap and refrigerate up to 4 days.

Substitution Tip: If berries aren't your thing, substitute ½ banana, sliced, or 1 tablespoon chocolate chips.

CONTINUED

Berry Pancakes in a Jar CONTINUED

5. When you're ready to cook, remove the plastic wrap and microwave at 70 percent power for 2 minutes. If the center is still wet and gooey, continue to bake in 20-second intervals until the top is spongy and cakelike.
6. Top with more berries and serve with maple syrup (if using)—syrup does make everything better.

PER SERVING: Calories: 180; Total fat: 3g; Carbohydrates: 32g; Fiber: 1g; Protein: 7g

Blueberry Muffin in a Mug

It's pretty much impossible to have a bad day when you start it with this muffin. Just about any berries—fresh or frozen—will work here, and you can skip the streusel, but I wouldn't recommend it. This caramelized topping is too good to pass up.

MICROWAVE

15 MINUTES OR LESS

VEGETARIAN

Serves 1

PREP TIME
10 minutes

COOK TIME
2 minutes

Substitution Tip: You can use granulated white sugar, but brown sugar results in a richer, more caramelized flavor.

FOR THE MUFFIN BATTER

⅓ cup all-purpose flour

¼ teaspoon baking powder

¼ teaspoon salt

2 tablespoons light brown sugar

2 tablespoons melted unsalted butter

¼ teaspoon vanilla extract

¼ cup water

¼ cup fresh or frozen blueberries

FOR THE STREUSEL

2 teaspoons all-purpose flour

1 tablespoon light brown sugar

⅛ teaspoon ground cinnamon

1 tablespoon cold unsalted butter, diced

TO MAKE THE MUFFIN BATTER

In a mug, combine the flour, baking powder, and salt. Stir in the brown sugar, melted butter, and vanilla. Add the water and stir until smooth. Using a silicone spatula, fold in the blueberries.

CONTINUED

Blueberry Muffin in a Mug CONTINUED

TO MAKE THE STREUSEL

1. In a small bowl, combine the flour, brown sugar, and cinnamon. Add the butter and, using a fork, mix it in, breaking up the mixture to form small crumbles. Sprinkle the streusel over the batter in the mug.
2. Microwave the muffin for about 1½ minutes, or until lightly golden. You may need another 30 seconds, depending on how powerful your microwave is.

MAKE IT VEGAN: Swap coconut oil for the butter in both the batter and streusel.

PER SERVING: Calories: 605; Total fat: 35g; Carbohydrates: 69g; Fiber: 3g; Protein: 6g

COOKIES AND CRÈME POPCORN
(PAGE 38)

chapter 3

SWEET AND SAVORY SNACKS

Big Dill Feta Dip

NO COOK

15 MINUTES OR LESS

ONE BOWL

VEGETARIAN

Serves 2

PREP TIME
10 minutes

Ingredient Tip: If you can't find fresh dill, the dried version is fine. The flavor won't be as strong, but it'll get the job done.

Modeled after tzatziki, a yogurt-cucumber sauce found on gyros and other Greek dishes, this dip makes a refreshing snack on scorching days. Its tangy flavor makes it great for savory entrées, like burgers and grilled chicken.

1 (5.3-ounce) container plain Greek yogurt

Juice of ½ lemon

1 teaspoon chopped fresh dill

½ teaspoon garlic powder

¼ teaspoon salt

½ cup crumbled feta cheese

1 cucumber, cut into slices

Cherry tomatoes, for serving

1. In a medium bowl, stir together the yogurt, lemon juice, dill, garlic powder, and salt.
2. Using a silicone spatula, fold in the feta cheese.
3. Serve with cucumber slices and cherry tomatoes for dipping.

PER SERVING: Calories: 147; Total fat: 7g; Carbohydrates: 12.6g; Fiber: 3g; Protein: 14g

Guacamole for Two

This recipe makes just enough guac for you and your roommate, though, after one bite, you may find it hard to share. If you're feeling fancy, stir in 1 teaspoon of fresh cilantro—provided neither of you has the gene that makes you sensitive to aldehydes (which makes the herb taste like soap).

NO COOK

15 MINUTES OR LESS

ONE BOWL

VEGAN

Serves 2

PREP TIME
10 minutes

1 avocado, halved and pitted

Juice of ½ lime

¼ teaspoon hot sauce, plus more, as needed

⅛ teaspoon salt

⅛ teaspoon pepper

1 tablespoon diced onion

4 to 5 cherry tomatoes, chopped (or ½ plum tomato, chopped)

Tortilla chips, carrot sticks, or sliced zucchini, for serving

1. Scoop the avocado flesh into a medium bowl. Using a spoon, mash the avocado.
2. Add the lime juice, hot sauce, salt, and pepper and stir well to combine.
3. Stir in the onion and cherry tomatoes. Serve with your choice of tortilla chips, carrot sticks, or zucchini.

PER SERVING: (GUACAMOLE ONLY) Calories: 174; Total fat: 11g; Carbohydrates: 19g; Fiber: 8g; Protein: 4g

Substitution Tip: Dice ½ jalapeño pepper instead of hot sauce and stir it into the guacamole for a more authentic jolt of heat (and some extra crunch).

Jalapeño Popper Dip

TOASTER OVEN

30 MINUTES OR LESS

Serves 8 to 10

PREP TIME
5 minutes

COOK TIME
20 minutes

Preparation Tip: Save time by buying a can of diced jalapeños instead of using fresh. Whichever you choose, wash your hands thoroughly afterward and don't rub jalapeño juice in your eyes (like I did).

If you're headed to a tailgate or watch party, bring this dip. It's an easy, quick-to-make crowd-pleaser and way less of a hassle than making actual jalapeño poppers. Bring tortilla chips, sliced zucchini, carrots, and celery sticks to use as dippers.

- **1 (8-ounce) package cream cheese, at room temperature**
- **½ cup sour cream**
- **1 teaspoon garlic powder**
- **2 cups shredded sharp Cheddar cheese, divided**
- **3 tablespoons diced jalapeño pepper**
- **4 cooked bacon slices, crumbled** **(see page 20)**

1. Preheat the toaster oven to 350°F.
2. In a medium bowl, stir together the cream cheese, sour cream, and garlic powder.
3. Set aside ¼ cup of Cheddar cheese for topping the dip.
4. Add the remaining Cheddar cheese, the jalapeño, and bacon to the cream cheese mixture and stir to combine. Scrape the mixture into an oven-safe casserole dish that fits in your toaster oven. Top with the reserved Cheddar cheese.
5. Bake for 15 to 20 minutes, or until the dip is bubbly and the cheese has melted.

PER SERVING: Calories: 251; Total fat: 21g; Carbohydrates: 5g; Fiber: 1g; Protein: 10g

Honey–Peanut Butter Banana Bites

Toss these little bites in a resealable bag and bring them to your next class for a snack. They are the perfect treat—no mess, no strong smells, and no loud crunching. Hey, you can't control when you'll get hangry. Best to stay prepared.

NO COOK

5-INGREDIENT

15 MINUTES OR LESS

VEGETARIAN

Serves 1

PREP TIME
5 minutes

1 whole-wheat tortilla

2 tablespoons peanut butter, crunchy or smooth

1 teaspoon honey

1 banana

1. Place the tortilla on a work surface. Spread the peanut butter over the tortilla and drizzle it with honey.
2. Place the banana at one edge of the tortilla and roll it up. Cut the rolled-up tortilla crosswise into 1-inch pieces, resembling sushi rolls.

PER SERVING: Calories: 198; Total fat: 9g; Carbohydrates: 26g; Fiber: 5g; Protein: 8g

Substitution Tip: If you don't do honey, try sweetening the snack with a drizzle of maple syrup or agave syrup. Or skip the sweetener altogether.

Cookies and Crème Popcorn

MICROWAVE

5-INGREDIENT

15 MINUTES OR LESS

VEGETARIAN

Serves 4 to 5

PREP TIME
5 minutes

COOK TIME
7 minutes

This salty-sweet snack is perfect for a late-night binge-watching session with your roommates. I recommend waiting to dig in until the chocolate has cooled to minimize the mess (and the popcorn will have a little crunch), but this kind of treat's hard to resist.

7 or 8 chocolate sandwich cookies

1 bag microwave popcorn

⅓ cup semisweet chocolate chips

1 teaspoon vegetable oil

1. Place the sandwich cookies in a resealable plastic bag. Seal the bag and use a spoon or a textbook to crush the cookies into fine crumbles.
2. Microwave the popcorn according to the package instructions. Transfer the popcorn to a large bowl, discarding any unpopped kernels.
3. In a small microwave-safe bowl, stir together the chocolate chips and vegetable oil and microwave for 20 to 25 seconds. Stir, then microwave in 20-second intervals until the chocolate has melted and is easy to drizzle.
4. Drizzle the chocolate over the popcorn, add the cookie crumbles, and toss until everything is evenly coated. Serve immediately, or spread into an even layer on a large plate and let cool so the chocolate can harden.

PER SERVING: Calories: 310; Total fat: 19g; Carbohydrates: 36g; Fiber: 4g; Protein: 4g

Apple Nachos

It's hard to make yourself sit down and write an essay—or spend the afternoon cramming for an exam—without the proper motivation. Apple nachos are a delicious way to fuel that marathon. You might even look forward to it!

MICROWAVE

5-INGREDIENT

15 MINUTES OR LESS

VEGETARIAN

Serves 1

PREP TIME
5 minutes

COOK TIME
15 seconds

- **1 tablespoon peanut butter, crunchy or smooth**
- **1 Granny Smith apple, cored and cut into slices**
- **1 graham cracker, crumbled**
- **1 tablespoon mini semisweet chocolate chips**

1. In a small microwave-safe bowl, microwave the peanut butter for 15 seconds and stir.
2. Arrange the apple slices on a plate. Drizzle with the melted peanut butter and sprinkle with graham cracker crumbles and the chocolate chips.

MAKE IT GLUTEN FREE: To make this snack gluten free, trade the graham cracker for chopped nuts and always remember to check packaging ingredients to ensure foods, especially oats and nuts, were processed in a completely gluten-free facility.

PER SERVING: Calories: 332; Total fat: 15g; Carbohydrates: 47g; Fiber: 7g; Protein: 6g

Substitution Tip: The beauty of these sweet nachos is that anything you have on hand could work here: Use almond butter, crumbled pretzels, chopped nuts, or dried fruit. Cacao nibs or coconut flakes are also nice.

English Muffin Pizza

TOASTER OVEN

5-INGREDIENT

15 MINUTES OR LESS

Serves 1

PREP TIME
5 minutes

COOK TIME
7 minutes

Substitution Tip: To boost the flavor in this dish, try sliced fresh mozzarella and chopped fresh basil. Suddenly, your toaster-oven treat will taste totally gourmet.

This pizza is simple, fast, and convenient and, as long as you keep an eye on it while it's cooking, you can't fail at making it. What are you waiting for?

1 English muffin, split
2 tablespoons marinara sauce
¼ teaspoon dried basil
¼ cup shredded mozzarella cheese
6 pepperoni slices

1. Preheat the toaster oven to 375°F.
2. Place both halves of the English muffin on the toaster oven tray, cut-side up. Spread 1 tablespoon of marinara on each half. Sprinkle the basil on top, and divide the mozzarella and pepperoni slices between the halves.
3. Bake for 5 to 7 minutes, or until the cheese has melted.

MAKE IT GLUTEN FREE: Choose gluten-free English muffins (like Udi® or Food for Life® brand) instead of traditional ones and always remember to check packaging ingredients to ensure foods, especially oats, were processed in a completely gluten-free facility.

PER SERVING: Calories: 265; Total fat: 11g; Carbohydrates: 31g; Fiber: 3g; Protein: 13g

Zesty Ranch Potato Tots

A packet of ranch seasoning, found in the salad dressing aisle of the grocery store, is an instant party starter. Mix it with sour cream and you've got ranch dip. Sprinkle a pinch on fries, hot popcorn, steam-in-bag microwave broccoli—it makes everything better. But it's best on tots with a zesty splash of lime juice.

TOASTER OVEN

5-INGREDIENT

30 MINUTES OR LESS

VEGAN

Serves 2

PREP TIME
5 minutes

COOK TIME
15 minutes

1¼ cups frozen potato tots
1 teaspoon ranch seasoning mix
¼ lime

1. Preheat the toaster oven to 450°F.
2. Place the potato tots in a large bowl and toss with the ranch seasoning until lightly coated. Arrange the tots in a single layer on the toaster oven tray.
3. Bake for 14 to 15 minutes, or until lightly golden.
4. Squeeze the lime juice over the top and serve.

Preparation Tip: If you have people coming over—and access to a full oven—triple this recipe, using the whole bag of tots. You may need to bake them for an extra 3 to 4 minutes, depending on how crowded the baking sheet is.

PER SERVING: Calories: 284; Total fat: 14g; Carbohydrates: 38g; Fiber: 4g; Protein: 4g

Pretzel Dogs

TOASTER OVEN

5-INGREDIENT

30 MINUTES OR LESS

Serves 4

PREP TIME
10 minutes

COOK TIME
20 minutes

Substitution Tip: Veggie dogs work just as well here. Swap 'em out and enjoy.

Pigs in a blanket have nothing on pretzel dogs. Sure, they require a bit more effort, but they're worth it.

½ can refrigerated biscuit dough (4 pieces; reserve the remaining biscuits in a resealable bag for another use)

Water, for cooking

¼ cup baking soda

4 hot dogs

Coarse sea salt

1. Preheat the toaster oven to 425°F.
2. On a clean surface and with clean hands, roll each piece of dough into a long snake shape. Wrap each dough snake around a hot dog in a spiral.
3. Fill a bowl, large enough to fit a wrapped hot dog, with water and microwave the water for 1 minute to heat it. Add the baking soda and stir until it dissolves.
4. Working one at a time, using tongs or two forks, submerge the wrapped hot dogs in the water-baking soda mixture for about 20 seconds. If the water cools to room temperature, microwave it for about 30 seconds to reheat before continuing.
5. Place as many wrapped, soaked dogs as will fit in the toaster oven tray, without touching, and sprinkle them with salt.
6. Bake for 15 to 17 minutes, or until the biscuit dough is golden.

PER SERVING: Calories: 165; Total fat: 14g; Carbohydrates: 5g; Fiber: 0g; Protein: 6g

PIZZA GRILLED CHEESE
(PAGE 48)

chapter 4

QUICK SANDWICHES AND WRAPS

Egg Salad Sandwich

HOT PLATE OR STOVETOP

TOASTER OVEN

5-INGREDIENT

30 MINUTES OR LESS

VEGETARIAN

Serves 1

PREP TIME
5 minutes

COOK TIME
10 minutes, plus 15 minutes cooling

Substitution Tip: For a breakfast-inspired twist, stir in a slice of cooked, crumbled bacon. Or, if you want a kick, add a pinch of cayenne pepper or a drizzle of hot sauce.

It's a classic for a reason: Egg salad's ridiculously easy to make and it's tasty, too. If you can boil water, you can make this meal. Yes, you can.

2 large eggs
Water, for cooking
1 tablespoon salt, plus more for seasoning
2 tablespoons mayonnaise
¼ teaspoon paprika
¼ teaspoon pepper
2 slices whole-wheat bread

1. Place the eggs in a saucepan and add enough water to cover the salt. Place the pan over high heat and bring the water to a boil. Cook the eggs for 7 to 8 minutes. Drain the water and let the eggs cool for 15 minutes.
2. Peel and chop the eggs.
3. In a medium bowl, stir together the mayonnaise, paprika, and pepper. Season to taste with salt. Add the chopped eggs and gently stir to mix.
4. Toast the bread in a toaster oven or toaster.
5. Top one slice of toast with half the egg salad. Top the second slice of toast with the remaining egg salad.

PER SERVING: Calories: 525; Total fat: 34g; Carbohydrates: 32g; Fiber: 5g; Protein: 22g

Caprese Wrap

Just because you're a vegetarian—or trying to go meatless more often—doesn't mean you're limited to PB&J sandwiches. The combo of herby pesto, creamy mozzarella, and tangy vinegar make this sandwich super satisfying. Look for prepared pesto at the grocery store.

NO COOK

5-INGREDIENT

15 MINUTES OR LESS

VEGETARIAN

Serves 1

PREP TIME
2 minutes

1 whole-wheat tortilla, or spinach tortilla

1 tablespoon pesto

3 tomato slices

¼ cup shredded mozzarella cheese

½ teaspoon balsamic vinegar

Place the tortilla on a work surface. Spread the pesto over the tortilla. Top with tomato slices and mozzarella. Drizzle with balsamic vinegar. Roll up the tortilla and serve.

MAKE IT GLUTEN FREE: Use a spinach tortilla and always remember to check packaging ingredients to ensure foods, especially oats, were processed in a completely gluten-free facility.

PER SERVING: Calories: 279; Total fat: 14g; Carbohydrates: 30g; Fiber: 4g; Protein: 11g

Substitution Tip: Cut a ball of fresh mozzarella into slices instead of the shredded stuff for a creamier texture and heartier meal overall. If you don't have or want to buy pesto, use a few leaves of basil instead.

Pizza Grilled Cheese

HOT PLATE OR STOVETOP

15 MINUTES OR LESS

Serves 1

PREP TIME
3 minutes

COOK TIME
4 minutes

Technique Tip: If you like your sandwich to be more golden brown, try spreading mayonnaise instead of butter on the bread, which browns more evenly.

Just when you thought grilled cheese couldn't get any better, it gets pizza-fied. Any of your favorite pizza toppings can be thrown in here, so don't limit yourself to pepperoni. (If you're adding meat, though, make sure it's already cooked.)

1 tablespoon unsalted butter, at room temperature

2 slices whole-wheat bread, or white bread

2 tablespoons marinara sauce

⅓ cup shredded mozzarella cheese, divided

1 teaspoon finely grated Parmesan cheese, divided

6 slices pepperoni

1. Spread the butter on one side of each slice of bread. Spread the marinara on the other side of each slice. Place one slice of bread, butter-side down, on a cutting board and sprinkle it with half the mozzarella cheese and half the Parmesan cheese. Add a layer of pepperoni slices. Sprinkle on the remaining mozzarella and Parmesan and top with the other slice of bread, butter-side up.
2. Heat a skillet over medium heat. Place the sandwich in the pan and cook for about 2 minutes until lightly golden. Using a spatula, flip the sandwich and cook for 1 to 2 minutes more, or until the bread is lightly golden and the cheese has melted.
3. Halve the sandwich and serve.

MAKE IT VEGETARIAN: Omit the pepperoni—easy as that.

PER SERVING: Calories: 394; Total fat: 25g; Carbohydrates: 29g; Fiber: 2g; Protein: 15g

Turkey BLT Wrap

Whether sandwiched between two slices of bread or rolled in a tortilla, you can't go wrong with this flavor combo. The bacon and turkey amp up the salty, smoky flavor; the mayo adds a creamy texture; the produce provides a little crunch—it all works.

MICROWAVE

15 MINUTES OR LESS

Serves 1

PREP TIME
5 minutes

COOK TIME
1 minute

1 bacon slice, halved widthwise

1 whole-wheat tortilla

1 teaspoon mayonnaise, or ranch dressing

⅛ teaspoon pepper

1 butter lettuce leaf, or any lettuce you have on hand

½ plum tomato, sliced

3 slices smoked turkey breast

1. Place the bacon on a microwave-safe plate lined with paper towels. Microwave for 1 minute, or until lightly crispy.
2. Place the tortilla on a work surface. Spread the mayonnaise on one side of the tortilla. Season with pepper. Top with lettuce, tomato slices, turkey, and the bacon. Roll up the tortilla and enjoy immediately.

MAKE IT GLUTEN FREE: Wrap the sandwich in the lettuce instead of using a tortilla and always remember to check packaging ingredients to ensure foods, especially oats, were processed in a completely gluten-free facility.

PER SERVING: Calories: 278; Total fat: 10g; Carbohydrates: 28g; Fiber: 5g; Protein: 20g

Preparation Tip: If you're meal prepping, slice the tomato, tear the lettuce, cook the bacon, and refrigerate all three ingredients in resealable plastic bags. Don't assemble the sandwiches more than 2 hours ahead of time—the tortilla will get soggy and the lettuce will wilt.

Turkey Reuben

MICROWAVE

HOT PLATE OR STOVETOP

15 MINUTES OR LESS

Serves 1

PREP TIME
2 minutes

COOK TIME
6 minutes

Sauerkraut, Thousand Island dressing, Swiss cheese—a Reuben doesn't seem like it should taste as good as it does. But then you try one—and your mind is blown. It's salty, tangy, cheesy—basically, everything you crave in a single bite.

- **¼ cup sauerkraut, drained**
- **1½ teaspoons unsalted butter, at room temperature**
- **2 slices rye bread**
- **1 tablespoon Thousand Island dressing**
- **2 slices Swiss cheese**
- **4 slices smoked turkey**

1. Place the sauerkraut in a small microwave-safe bowl and microwave for 30 seconds. Set aside.
2. Spread the butter on one side of each slice of bread. Spread the Thousand Island dressing on the other side of each slice of bread. Place one slice of bread, butter-side down on a cutting board. Layer with 1 slice of cheese, the turkey, sauerkraut, and the other slice of cheese. Top with the remaining slice of bread, butter-side up.
3. Heat a skillet over medium heat. Place the sandwich in the skillet and cook for about 3 minutes until the bread is lightly golden and the cheese has started to melt. Using a spatula, gently flip the sandwich and cook for 1 to 2 minutes more until golden.

PER SERVING: Calories: 503; Total fat: 27g; Carbohydrates: 39g; Fiber: 5g; Protein: 27g

Buffalo Chicken Salad Sandwich

Regular chicken salad is fine . . . until you've tried it buffalo style. This recipe is the perfect way to use leftover chicken—enjoy a hot-from-the-grocery-store rotisserie chicken with vegetables one night and have it for lunch the next day. No harm, no (left-over) fowl.

NO COOK

15 MINUTES OR LESS

Serves 2

PREP TIME
15 minutes

- **½ rotisserie chicken, shredded or cut into bite-size pieces**
- **¼ cup mayonnaise**
- **2 tablespoons buffalo sauce**
- **1 celery stalk, diced**
- **1 teaspoon diced scallion**
- **Salt**
- **Pepper**
- **4 slices whole-wheat bread, or white bread**

1. In a medium bowl, stir together the chicken, mayonnaise, and buffalo sauce, 1 tablespoon at a time, stirring in between, until you reach your preferred consistency.
2. Add the celery and scallion and stir to combine. Season with salt and pepper, to taste.
3. Spread the chicken salad onto 2 slices of bread. Top with the remaining slices, halve each sandwich, and serve.

MAKE IT GLUTEN FREE: The filling has enough flavor that you can easily ditch the bread and wrap it in a leaf of romaine, iceberg, or butter lettuce and always remember to check packaging ingredients to ensure foods, especially oats, were processed in a completely gluten-free facility.

Substitution Tip: Use shredded canned chicken—or boil a chicken breast in a saucepan until it's no longer pink when you cut into it with a knife, about 15 minutes—in place of rotisserie chicken.

PER SERVING: (1 SANDWICH) Calories: 384; Total fat: 12g; Carbohydrates: 45g; Fiber: 2g; Protein: 38g

Shortcut Cuban Sandwiches

HOT PLATE OR STOVETOP

15 MINUTES OR LESS

Serves 2

PREP TIME
10 minutes

COOK TIME
5 minutes

Preparation Tip: Look for precooked, shredded pork in the meat department of the grocery store—a barbecued pulled pork can work nicely (but only if the sauce comes in a separate packet—you can save it for another meal and slather the meat with the mojo sauce instead).

Despite its name, the Cuban sandwich originated in Tampa, Florida, not Cuba. It's like a toasted ham and cheese sandwich taken to the next level. This version takes a few liberties, so feel free to adjust the recipe to suit your tastes. Whatever you do, don't ditch the mojo marinade—a citrusy sauce that tenderizes the pork, infusing the whole sandwich with irresistibly tangy flavor. You can find it in the international food aisle of most grocery stores.

8 ounces cooked roast pork, shredded or chopped

¼ cup bottled mojo pork marinade

1 tablespoon unsalted butter, at room temperature

1 small loaf French bread, halved lengthwise

1 tablespoon yellow mustard

4 slices Swiss cheese

4 slices deli ham

Dill pickles, to taste

1. In a medium bowl, toss together the roast pork and mojo marinade. Set aside.
2. Spread the butter on the crust side of each piece of bread. Spread the mustard on the cut side of each piece of bread. Layer half the cheese over the mustard, then add the ham, pork, pickles, and the remaining cheese slices. Close the sandwich, mustard-side down.

3. Heat a skillet over medium heat. Place the sandwich in the skillet and cook for about 3 minutes, pressing it down with a spatula or the bottom of a clean skillet, until the cheese is melted. Flip the sandwich and cook for 1 to 2 minutes more until golden brown.

PER SERVING: Calories: 620; Total fat: 29g; Carbohydrates: 32g; Fiber: 2g; Protein: 58g

Meatball Subs

MICROWAVE

TOASTER OVEN

5-INGREDIENT

15 MINUTES OR LESS

Serves 2

PREP TIME
5 minutes

COOK TIME
10 minutes

Preparation Tip: You can bake subs for a group by baking the meatballs and marinara in a casserole dish in a 350°F oven until heated through. Fill the buns and place the filled sandwiches on a baking sheet, top with cheese, and continue baking until the cheese starts to melt, about 5 minutes.

Frozen meatballs are the fastest way to make this recipe but if you're looking for something a little more homemade, make the Mozzarella-Stuffed Meatballs (page 93) and use them here. Because you really can't go wrong with more cheese.

2 cups marinara sauce
8 to 10 frozen Italian meatballs
2 hoagie rolls
4 slices provolone cheese

1. Preheat the toaster oven to 350°F.
2. Pour the marinara into a medium microwave-safe bowl and add the meatballs. Cover and microwave for about 1 minute for every 3 meatballs, or until heated through.
3. Slice the hoagie rolls lengthwise, without cutting all the way through (so it opens like a hot dog bun). Place a line of meatballs down the center of each sandwich roll. Spoon marinara over the meatballs and top each sandwich with 2 slices of provolone.
4. Place the sandwiches in the toaster oven and bake for about 5 minutes until the cheese melts.

PER SERVING: Calories: 731; Total fat: 37g; Carbohydrates: 69g; Fiber: 7g; Protein: 34g

Roast Beef and Cheddar Sandwich

There's a certain fast-food chain that's famous for its hot roast beef and Cheddar sandwiches. And—dare I say it?—these are even better. (Triple the cheese sauce, and you've got a quick queso for parties, BTW.)

HOT PLATE OR STOVETOP

TOASTER OVEN

15 MINUTES OR LESS

Serves 2

PREP TIME
5 minutes

COOK TIME
15 minutes

Technique Tip: Whisking the sauce constantly as you add ingredients is crucial to creating a cheese sauce that's smooth. When you first add the milk, the mixture will look clumpy and congealed, but keep stirring—it'll come together.

FOR THE SANDWICHES

2 onion rolls, halved horizontally

1 tablespoon unsalted butter, at room temperature

8 ounces sliced deli roast beef

FOR THE CHEESE SAUCE

1 tablespoon unsalted butter

1 tablespoon all-purpose flour

½ cup whole milk

⅓ cup shredded sharp Cheddar cheese

¼ teaspoon chili powder

TO MAKE THE SANDWICHES

1. Preheat the toaster oven to 375°F.
2. Slather the insides of each roll with butter. Divide the roast beef between the two bottom halves of the rolls.
3. Place them on the toaster oven tray and warm in the toaster oven for 3 to 5 minutes.

CONTINUED

Roast Beef and Cheddar Sandwich CONTINUED

TO MAKE THE CHEESE SAUCE

1. In a saucepan over medium heat, melt the butter. Whisk in the flour, creating a paste. Slowly pour in the milk while whisking constantly until blended.
2. Whisk in the cheese and the chili powder and cook, whisking, until the cheese melts and creates a smooth sauce.
3. Remove the rolls from the toaster oven. Drizzle the cheese sauce over the roast beef. Top with the remaining roll halves and serve.

PER SERVING: Calories: 469; Total fat: 22g; Carbohydrates: 34g; Fiber: 2g; Protein: 33g

ASIAN CHICKEN SALAD
(PAGE 66)

chapter 5

SIMPLE SALADS

Greek Pasta Salad

HOT PLATE OR STOVETOP

VEGETARIAN

Serves 3

PREP TIME
5 minutes, plus one hour chilling

COOK TIME
10 minutes

Substitution Tip: If you can't find a plum tomato, toss in some halved cherry tomatoes or a handful of grape tomatoes.

If you're heading to a cookout or potluck, this recipe's pretty foolproof—and is a fresh take on all those traditional pasta salads dripping in mayo. If kept refrigerated, the salad can last a few days, and it tastes better the longer the flavors meld.

Water, for cooking

½ (16-ounce) package bow-tie pasta, or cavatappi pasta

1 plum tomato, diced

⅓ cup feta cheese

¼ cup halved Kalamata olives

½ cucumber, diced

½ cup Greek vinaigrette dressing

Salt

1. Fill a saucepan with water and bring to a boil over high heat. Add the pasta and cook until al dente, according to the package instructions. Drain the pasta and transfer to a large bowl.
2. Add the tomato, feta cheese, olives, cucumber, and dressing to the pasta and toss to combine. Season with salt, to taste.
3. Transfer the mixture to an airtight container and refrigerate at least 1 hour to give the flavors a chance to meld.

MAKE IT VEGAN: Omit the feta cheese.

PER SERVING: Calories: 273; Total fat: 17g; Carbohydrates: 25g; Fiber: 3g; Protein: 7g

Tropical Fruit Salad

If you don't have a kitchen but you need to prepare a dish to bring to a tailgate, this is it. All the fresh fruit is insanely refreshing on scorching game days. Make it the night before and you'll be ready to be the MVP of your party.

NO COOK

5-INGREDIENT

15 MINUTES OR LESS

ONE BOWL

VEGAN

Serves 4 to 6

PREP TIME
15 minutes

¼ mini seedless watermelon, cut into ½-inch chunks (about 2 cups)

½ (20-ounce) can pineapple chunks, drained

1 mango, peeled and diced

6 or 7 strawberries, hulled and cut into slices

Juice of 1 lime

1. In a large bowl or airtight container, stir together the watermelon, pineapple, mango, and strawberries. Add the lime juice and toss to coat.
2. Store the fruit salad in an airtight container and refrigerate for at least 20 minutes before serving.

PER SERVING: Calories: 137; Total fat: 1g; Carbohydrates: 38g; Fiber: 4g; Protein: 2g

Substitution Tip: This salad is versatile. No watermelon? Try cantaloupe or honeydew melon. Can't find a mango? Grab two mandarin oranges.

Lemon-Garlic Kale Salad

NO COOK

30 MINUTES OR LESS

VEGETARIAN

Serves 2

PREP TIME
15 minutes, plus 15 minutes chilling

Preparation Tip: If you're saving the other salad bowl for later, cover and refrigerate and don't add the dressing until you're ready to serve.

The citrus-garlic-salt trifecta really makes this salad. If you've never liked kale, you'll likely change your mind when you try this.

FOR THE DRESSING

¼ cup freshly squeezed lemon juice

¾ cup olive oil

1 teaspoon minced garlic

⅛ teaspoon salt

FOR THE SALAD

1 (10-ounce) package kale, stemmed and torn into bite-size pieces

⅓ cup shredded Parmesan cheese

2 carrots, peeled and diced

TO MAKE THE DRESSING

In a jar with a lid, combine the lemon juice, olive oil, garlic, and salt. Seal the lid and shake vigorously to blend the dressing. Refrigerate the dressing for at least 15 minutes.

TO MAKE THE SALAD

Divide the kale into 2 large bowls. Divide the cheese and carrots between each bowl. If eating right away, drizzle the salads with the dressing and toss to coat.

PER SERVING: Calories: 488; Total fat: 46g; Carbohydrates: 11g; Fiber: 4g

Quinoa Spinach Salad

If you're looking for a classic vinaigrette to top any salad, look no further. It's just the right mix of salt, fat, and acid to liven up any combination of greens. Here, it works especially well to amp up the good-for-you flavors of spinach and quinoa.

NO COOK

15 MINUTES OR LESS

ONE BOWL

VEGAN

Serves 1

PREP TIME
15 minutes

FOR THE VINAIGRETTE

2 tablespoons olive oil

1½ tablespoons red wine vinegar

1½ teaspoons freshly squeezed lemon juice

¼ teaspoon garlic powder

¼ teaspoon salt

FOR THE SALAD

2 carrots, peeled and cut into coins

1 red bell pepper, seeded and diced

1½ cups fresh spinach

½ cup cooked quinoa

TO MAKE THE VINAIGRETTE

In a medium bowl, whisk the olive oil, vinegar, lemon juice, garlic powder, and salt until combined.

TO MAKE THE SALAD

To the dressing, add the carrots, red bell pepper, spinach, and quinoa and toss until coated.

PER SERVING: Calories: 468; Total fat: 30g; Carbohydrates: 44g; Fiber: 11g; Protein: 8g

Preparation Tip: Cook a big batch of quinoa and refrigerate it in an airtight container so you'll have some ready whenever you need it. Several brands make single-serving microwaveable quinoa, too, which is nice to keep in your makeshift pantry.

Strawberry Pecan Salad

TOASTER OVEN

15 MINUTES OR LESS

VEGETARIAN

Serves 1

PREP TIME
10 minutes

COOK TIME
5 minutes

Substitution Tip: If you're not into blue cheese, try feta cheese, which will add a little saltiness to offset the sweetness of the strawberries and a bit of a creamy texture.

Toasting the pecans brings out their nutty flavor and they taste great paired with the sweet-tart flavors of the strawberries and balsamic vinaigrette.

¼ cup chopped pecans

1 teaspoon olive oil

½ (8-ounce) bag fresh spinach

6 or 7 fresh strawberries, hulled and cut into slices

¼ red onion, diced

2 tablespoons crumbled blue cheese

Balsamic vinaigrette, for serving

1. Preheat the toaster oven to 350°F.
2. In a small bowl, toss the pecans in the olive oil and spread them in an even layer on the toaster oven tray.
3. Bake for 4 minutes, or until they are lightly browned and start to smell nutty.
4. In a large bowl, toss together the spinach, strawberries, red onion, and blue cheese. Top with the nuts and drizzle with the vinaigrette.

PER SERVING: Calories: 499; Total fat: 42g; Carbohydrates: 25g; Fiber: 9g; Protein: 13g

Roasted Sweet Potato Salad

This salad combines all the best fall flavors into one bowl, but it's so addictive you'll want to make it year-round—and that's just fine.

TOASTER OVEN

30 MINUTES OR LESS

VEGETARIAN

Serves 4

PREP TIME
10 minutes

COOK TIME
20 minutes, plus cooling

2 sweet potatoes, peeled and cut into cubes

Olive oil

Salt

Pepper

1 Granny Smith, Fuji, or Gala apple, cored, and diced

1 (8- to 10-ounce) bag spring greens mix

¼ cup crumbled goat cheese

Balsamic vinaigrette, for serving

1. Preheat the toaster oven to 425°F.
2. Place the sweet potatoes on the toaster oven tray, drizzle with oil, and season with salt and pepper, to taste.
3. Bake for 18 to 20 minutes, or until tender when pierced with a fork. Let cool.
4. In a medium bowl, toss the sweet potatoes with the apples and spring mix. Divide the salad into 4 airtight containers and refrigerate.
5. When ready to serve, add 1 tablespoon of goat cheese to each salad and drizzle with the vinaigrette.

MAKE IT VEGAN: Omit the goat cheese.

PER SERVING: Calories: 204; Total fat: 9g; Carbohydrates: 24g; Fiber: 5g; Protein: 4g

Preparation Tip: Roast the sweet potatoes ahead of time and refrigerate them in an airtight container so you can keep them on hand to enjoy this salad throughout the week.

Asian Chicken Salad

TOASTER OVEN

5-INGREDIENT

Serves 2

PREP TIME
15 minutes, plus 15 minutes marinating

COOK TIME
25 minutes

Substitution Tip: For a vegan salad, trade the chicken for roasted chickpeas, sweet potatoes, or cooked quinoa.

Bagged coleslaw is one of the cheapest salad mixes you can buy. The lettuce, carrots, and cabbage are pre-shredded, so all you have to do is cook the chicken and whisk the dressing.

2 boneless, skinless chicken breasts

1 (16-ounce) bottle Asian sesame vinaigrette, divided

1 tablespoon creamy peanut butter

1 (14-ounce) bag coleslaw mix

4 scallions, chopped

1. Place the chicken in a large bowl or a large resealable plastic bag and pour in half the vinaigrette. Seal the bag and refrigerate to marinate for 15 minutes.
2. Preheat the toaster oven to 350°F.
3. In another large bowl, whisk the remaining vinaigrette and peanut butter until smooth. Set aside.
4. Remove the chicken from the bag, shaking off any excess vinaigrette, and place it on the toaster oven tray.
5. Bake for 20 to 25 minutes, or until the chicken is no longer pink when you cut into it with a knife.
6. Using two forks, shred the chicken into small pieces and add it to the bowl with the peanut butter vinaigrette.
7. Add the coleslaw mix and scallions and toss to combine. Divide the salad onto 2 plates and serve.

PER SERVING: Calories: 534; Total fat: 18g; Carbohydrates: 32g; Fiber: 8g; Protein: 66g

Chicken Bacon Ranch Salad

Chicken, bacon, and ranch are the holy trinity of twenty-first century food. It's amazing how three, kind of ordinary, ingredients can transform romaine lettuce into an epic salad.

MICROWAVE

HOT PLATE OR STOVETOP

30 MINUTES OR LESS

Serves 2

PREP TIME
15 minutes

COOK TIME
15 minutes, plus cooling

1 boneless, skinless chicken breast
Water, for cooking
4 bacon slices
½ head romaine lettuce, chopped
1 pint cherry tomatoes
3 carrots, peeled and cut into coins
1 cucumber, peeled and cut into coins
Ranch dressing, for serving

1. Place the chicken in a saucepan, add enough water to cover, and bring to a boil over high heat. Reduce the heat to medium-low, cover the pan with a lid, and simmer for about 15 minutes until the chicken is no longer pink when you cut into it with a knife. Transfer the chicken to a plate and let cool. Using two forks, shred the meat into small pieces.
2. While the chicken cooks, place the bacon on a microwave-safe plate lined with paper towels, keeping the slices just far enough apart that they aren't touching. Microwave for 4 minutes, check for doneness, and continue to microwave in 20-second intervals until you've reached your desired crispness. Chop the bacon.
3. Divide the romaine lettuce between 2 bowls. Top with the chicken, bacon, tomatoes, carrots, and cucumber. Drizzle with the ranch dressing.

Preparation Tip: Set yourself up for the week by tearing romaine into bite-size pieces, wrapping them in paper towels, and placing in an airtight container. The paper towels will absorb excess moisture and keep the lettuce from wilting.

PER SERVING: Calories: 416; Total fat: 17g; Carbohydrates: 26g; Fiber: 9g; Protein: 41g

Taco Salad

MICROWAVE

15 MINUTES OR LESS

Serves 2

PREP TIME
5 minutes

COOK TIME
10 minutes

Technique Tip: Stir 1 teaspoon of water and a pinch of leftover taco seasoning (or a few drops of hot sauce) into the sour cream to create a spiced *crema*. The thinner sauce will be easier to drizzle and it will give the salad an extra kick.

It may seem crazy to cook ground beef in the microwave, but don't let that stop you—it tastes as good as when cooked the conventional way. Rather than breaking up the meat as it cooks, as you would on a stovetop, chop it after it's done cooking.

- **8 ounces ground beef**
- **½ (1-ounce) packet taco seasoning**
- **¼ cup water**
- **½ (15-ounce) can black beans, drained and rinsed**
- **½ head romaine lettuce, chopped**
- **1 plum tomato, diced**
- **2 tablespoons shredded Mexican-style cheese blend**
- **2 tablespoons sour cream**
- **Crushed tortilla chips, for garnish**

1. Place the ground beef in a medium microwave-safe bowl and break it up with a spoon. Add the taco seasoning and water and toss to coat the meat. Form a well in the middle of the meat so it will cook more evenly. Microwave for 5 to 6 minutes, or until the meat is dark brown and no longer pink in the center. Use a clean spoon to break up the meat into smaller pieces.
2. Place the black beans in a small microwave-safe bowl and microwave for 1½ to 2 minutes.
3. Divide the lettuce between 2 bowls. Top with the beef mixture, beans, tomato, cheese, and a dollop of sour cream. Garnish with tortilla chips.

PER SERVING: Calories: 612; Total fat: 28g; Carbohydrates: 47g; Fiber: 16g; Protein: 43g

UPGRADED INSTANT RAMEN
(PAGE 77)

chapter 6

SUPER SOUPS

French Onion Soup

MICROWAVE

15 MINUTES OR LESS

ONE BOWL

Serves 2

PREP TIME
5 minutes

COOK TIME
10 minutes, plus 2 minutes resting

Substitution Tip: This recipe is a great way to make use of stale bread. Just about any type of bread will work, as long as it isn't sweet. Unless you're into that sort of thing.

If you thought onion soup was really all about the bread and cheese, try giving the onions a few minutes to caramelize in the microwave before adding the broth. The onions mellow out, turning into delicious low-carb, al dente "noodles."

- **1 tablespoon unsalted butter**
- **½ Vidalia onion, cut into slices**
- **2 cups low-sodium beef broth**
- **¼ cup water**
- **¼ teaspoon garlic powder**
- **Salt**
- **Pepper**
- **1 slice rye bread, or 1 slice French baguette, cut into pieces**
- **2 slices Swiss cheese, or provolone cheese**

1. Place the butter in a large microwave-safe bowl and microwave for 20 to 25 seconds, or until melted. Add the onion and stir to coat. Place a paper towel on top of the bowl (to catch splashes) and microwave for 3 minutes, or until the onion is translucent.
2. Add the beef broth, water, and garlic powder. Re-cover the bowl and microwave for 3 minutes more. Season with salt and pepper, to taste.
3. Ladle the soup into 2 bowls. Top with the bread pieces and cheese. Let sit for 2 minutes until the bread absorbs the broth and the cheese melts.

PER SERVING: Calories: 211; Total fat: 13g; Carbohydrates: 15g; Fiber: 2g; Protein: 10g

Fire-Roasted Vegetable Soup

On rainy days, when you just want to feel cozy, there's nothing better than this veggie-laden soup. It tastes like you spent hours roasting the vegetables, when, really, the process involves little more than a few chops of a knife and presses of a button.

MICROWAVE

15 MINUTES OR LESS

VEGAN

Serves 1

PREP TIME
10 minutes

COOK TIME
5 minutes

¼ yellow onion, diced
½ teaspoon minced garlic
1 tablespoon olive oil
½ (14.5-ounce) can fire-roasted diced tomatoes, drained
½ (4.5-ounce) can diced green chilies, drained (optional)
¾ cup frozen mixed vegetables, such as carrots, peas, and green beans
¾ cup low-sodium vegetable broth
¼ teaspoon dried thyme
Salt
Pepper

1. In a medium microwave-safe bowl, combine the onion, garlic, and olive oil and toss until the onion is coated in the oil. Microwave for 45 seconds.
2. Add the tomatoes, green chilies (if using), mixed vegetables, vegetable broth, and thyme and stir to combine. Cover with a microwave-safe plate and microwave for 2½ minutes, or until hot. Season with salt and pepper, to taste.

PER SERVING: Calories: 263; Total fat: 14g; Carbohydrates: 29g; Fiber: 8g; Protein: 9g

Preparation Tip: Instead of buying the tomatoes and green chilies separately, look for brands like Ro-Tel® that combine them in one can. The chilies aren't vital here—they just add a little heat to the soup.

Creamy Tomato Soup

HOT PLATE OR STOVETOP

30 MINUTES OR LESS

VEGETARIAN

Serves 2

PREP TIME
5 minutes

COOK TIME
25 minutes

Preparation Tip: Refrigerate any leftover soup in an airtight container. Pop the soup in the microwave for 2 minutes, or until heated through. Add the cheese (if using) and dig in.

Putting soup in a blender may seem like an unnecessary extra step, but it's the key to a smooth, creamy soup—without using any cream. This stuff's better than any tomato soup you can buy in a can, too.

- **2 tablespoons unsalted butter**
- **½ yellow onion, diced**
- **1 (28-ounce) can crushed tomatoes, drained**
- **1 cup low-sodium vegetable broth**
- **¼ teaspoon salt**
- **1 slice provolone cheese, halved (optional)**

1. In a medium saucepan over medium heat, melt the butter.
2. Add the onion and cook until tender, about 30 seconds.
3. Increase the heat to medium-high, add the tomatoes, vegetable broth, and salt and bring the soup to a boil. Reduce the heat to medium-low and let simmer, uncovered, for about 20 minutes.
4. Carefully transfer the soup to a blender, making sure to fill it no more than half full. You may need to blend the soup in batches. Cover with the lid and blend until smooth.
5. Return the blended soup to the pot to rewarm before serving and top with a piece of cheese (if using).

PER SERVING: Calories: 282; Total fat: 16g; Carbohydrates: 33g; Fiber: 8g; Protein: 10g

Chicken Tortilla Soup

You might be tempted to skip this soup's lime juice. What could it really add? SO MUCH. That squirt of juice adds a depth of flavor that makes the tomatoes and chicken and beans and cheese all shine on their own. Skip the cheese, if you must. Keep the lime.

HOT PLATE OR STOVETOP

ONE POT

30 MINUTES OR LESS

Serves 4

PREP TIME
10 minutes

COOK TIME
15 minutes

3 cups low-sodium chicken broth

1 (14.5-ounce) can fire-roasted tomatoes, drained

1 boneless, skinless chicken breast, cut into 1-inch pieces

1 (15-ounce) can black beans, drained and rinsed

Juice of 1 lime

Salt

Pepper

½ cup shredded Monterey Jack cheese, or pepper Jack cheese, for serving

Crushed tortilla chips, for serving

1. In a medium saucepan over medium-high heat, stir together the chicken broth and tomatoes and bring to a boil.
2. Add the chicken and black beans to the pan, cover the pan, reduce the heat to medium-low, and simmer for 10 to 12 minutes until the chicken is no longer pink when you cut into it with a knife.
3. Stir in the lime juice and season with salt and pepper, to taste. Ladle the soup into bowls and garnish with cheese and tortilla chips.

Substitution Tip: Make the recipe with vegetable broth, trade out the chicken for ½ cup of cooked quinoa, and you have a very nice vegetarian meal.

PER SERVING: Calories: 347; Total fat: 9g; Carbohydrates: 44g; Fiber: 14g; Protein: 21g

Lasagna Soup

HOT PLATE OR STOVETOP

ONE POT

VEGETARIAN

Serves 2

PREP TIME
15 minutes

COOK TIME
20 minutes

Substitution Tip: Instant ramen is a cheap, easy college staple but you can make this recipe with broken lasagna noodles instead if that's what you have on hand.

When you crave all the flavors of lasagna but don't want to spend hours making it, turn to this recipe. You won't believe how a little ricotta and instant ramen transform a simple soup into a creamy, cheesy, dangerously addictive meal.

2 tablespoons olive oil

½ yellow onion, diced

1 teaspoon minced garlic

1 (28-ounce) can crushed tomatoes, drained

1 (14.5-ounce) can low-sodium vegetable both, or low-sodium chicken broth

1¼ cups water

1 (3-ounce) package instant ramen noodles only (seasoning packet discarded)

1 teaspoon dried basil

Salt

Pepper

¼ cup part-skim ricotta

¼ cup shredded mozzarella cheese

1. In a medium saucepan over medium heat, heat the olive oil.
2. Add the onion and garlic and cook for about 30 seconds until fragrant. Add the tomatoes and cook for 5 minutes more.
3. Add the vegetable broth, water, and ramen noodles. Cook for 10 minutes. Stir in the basil and season with salt and pepper, to taste.
4. Ladle the soup into 2 bowls. Add a heaping spoonful of ricotta to each and sprinkle with mozzarella.

PER SERVING: Calories: 486; Total fat: 20g; Carbohydrates: 65g; Fiber: 9g; Protein: 18g

Upgraded Instant Ramen

If you don't eat instant ramen your freshman year, it's like you never even went to college. Just because it's the quintessential student food, doesn't mean you have to settle for something subpar. A softboiled egg and some veggies are the key to taking this dish from alright to amazing.

MICROWAVE

15 MINUTES OR LESS

VEGETARIAN

Serves 1

PREP TIME
5 minutes

COOK TIME
5 minutes

- **2 cups water, divided**
- **1 teaspoon white vinegar**
- **1 large egg**
- **1 (3-ounce) package instant ramen, any flavor**
- **¼ cup frozen mixed vegetables**
- **1 teaspoon low-sodium soy sauce**
- **Juice of ¼ lime**
- **1 tablespoon sliced scallion**

1. In a microwave-safe mug, combine ½ cup of water and the vinegar and crack the egg into it. Gently pierce the yolk with a fork so it doesn't explode while cooking. Microwave at 80 percent power for 50 to 55 seconds. Drain the water and set aside.
2. In a microwave-safe soup bowl, combine the ramen noodles, mixed vegetables, and the remaining 1½ cups of water, submerging the ramen without the water reaching all the way to the bowl's rim. Cover the noodles with a microwave-safe plate and cook for 2½ minutes, or until the noodles are soft and loose.
3. Stir in half the ramen seasoning packet (save the other half for when you want to make this again), soy sauce, and lime juice. Top with the egg and scallion.

Fun Fact: Vinegar helps firm the egg whites so they won't spread into the water. If you cook the egg for 40 to 45 seconds, you'll end up with more of a poached egg, if a runny yolk is not your thing.

PER SERVING: Calories: 483; Total fat: 20g; Carbohydrates: 59g; Fiber: 5g; Protein: 18g

Chicken Ramen Noodle Soup

MICROWAVE

15 MINUTES OR LESS

ONE BOWL

Serves 1

PREP TIME
5 minutes

COOK TIME
5 minutes

Ingredient Tip: Take this soup to the next level of delicious with a little lemon juice. A squirt of tangy citrus livens up the whole dish, making the soup taste like you spent hours cooking it . . . even if you really spent 5 minutes.

Homesickness—or just plain regular ol' sickness—happens. And when it does, nothing comforts like classic chicken noodle soup. Here's the fastest way to get that flavor without resorting to the canned stuff.

½ carrot, peeled and diced
½ celery stalk, diced
Nonstick cooking spray
½ (3-ounce) package instant ramen, noodles only (seasoning packet discarded)
1 (14.5-ounce) can low-sodium chicken broth
¼ teaspoon garlic powder
1 teaspoon thinly sliced scallion
½ cup chopped rotisserie chicken, or leftover cooked chicken

1. In a medium microwave-safe bowl, combine the carrot and celery. Lightly coat the vegetables with cooking spray and microwave for 45 seconds.
2. Break the ramen noodles into small pieces and add them to the bowl, along with the chicken broth, garlic powder, scallion, and chicken. Cover the bowl and microwave for 2½ to 3 minutes, or until the noodles are tender and the soup is heated through.

PER SERVING: Calories: 401; Total fat: 18g; Carbohydrates: 30g; Fiber: 2g; Protein: 29g

Broccoli Cheddar Soup

Because this recipe requires a little more effort, make a larger batch so you can enjoy it for a few days (or split it with your roommate, and they can owe you one).

HOT PLATE OR STOVETOP

VEGETARIAN

Serves 4

PREP TIME
15 minutes

COOK TIME
20 minutes

- **3 tablespoons olive oil**
- **½ yellow onion, diced**
- **½ cup chopped peeled carrot**
- **2 teaspoons minced garlic**
- **1 head broccoli, stems removed and head cut into florets**
- **2 ounces cream cheese**
- **2 cups low-sodium vegetable broth, or low-sodium chicken broth**
- **1 cup milk**
- **1½ cups shredded sharp Cheddar cheese, plus more for topping**
- **Salt**
- **Pepper**

1. In a medium saucepan over medium heat, warm the olive oil.
2. Add the onion and carrot and cook for about 1 minute until the onion is slightly translucent.
3. Add the garlic and broccoli and cook for 2 to 3, stirring occasionally.
4. Add the cream cheese and cook, tossing with the vegetables, while the cheese melts.
5. Stir in the vegetable broth and milk and simmer the soup for 10 minutes.

CONTINUED

Preparation Tip: Use only the florets to make this soup. The stems are a little too crunchy and fibrous for it. Instead, chop the stems into bite-size pieces, toss with olive oil, salt, and pepper and roast them in your toaster oven at 425°F for 18 to 20 minutes, or until the edges have browned and the stems are tender when pierced with a fork. Makes a great side dish or snack.

Broccoli Cheddar Soup CONTINUED

6. A handful at a time, add the Cheddar cheese, stirring constantly until melted and combined. Season with salt and pepper, to taste.
7. For a creamier texture, carefully transfer the soup to a blender, making sure to fill it no more than half full. You may need to blend the soup in batches. Cover with the lid and blend until smooth.
8. Return the blended soup to the pot to rewarm before serving.

PER SERVING: Calories: 406; Total fat: 30g; Carbohydrates: 19g; Fiber: 6g; Protein: 17g

Loaded Cauliflower Soup

A little cheese and bacon go a long way in this ultra-rich, ultra-creamy soup.

MICROWAVE

30 MINUTES OR LESS

Serves 2

PREP TIME
10 minutes

COOK TIME
15 minutes

- **1 head cauliflower, chopped into florets**
- **Water, for cooking**
- **1½ cups low-sodium chicken broth, or low-sodium vegetable broth**
- **⅓ cup heavy (whipping) cream**
- **1 teaspoon garlic powder**
- **¼ teaspoon salt**
- **⅛ teaspoon pepper**
- **4 bacon slices**
- **⅓ cup shredded sharp Cheddar cheese**
- **1 teaspoon chopped fresh chives**

1. In a medium microwave-safe bowl, combine the cauliflower and just enough water to cover the bottom of the bowl. Cover the bowl with a paper towel and microwave for 5 minutes. Transfer the cauliflower and water to a blender, making sure to fill it no more than half full. You may need to blend the cauliflower in batches. Cover with the lid and blend until smooth. If necessary, add some of the chicken broth to blend the cauliflower properly. Pour the puréed cauliflower into a large microwave-safe bowl.
2. Stir in the chicken broth, heavy cream, garlic powder, salt, and pepper.

CONTINUED

Loaded Cauliflower Soup CONTINUED

3. Place the bacon on a microwave-safe plate lined with paper towels, keeping the slices just far enough apart that they aren't touching. Microwave for 4 minutes, check for doneness, and continue to microwave in 20-second intervals until you've reached your desired crispness. When cool enough to handle, crumble the bacon, set aside a small amount for topping, and stir the rest into the soup.
4. Cover the soup and microwave for 2 to 3 minutes, or until warm. Sprinkle with the Cheddar cheese, chives, and reserved bacon.

PER SERVING: Calories: 433; Total fat: 29g; Carbohydrates: 25g; Fiber: 9g; Protein: 23g

EASY BEEF BIBIMBAP
(PAGE 103)

chapter 7

RICE, NOODLES, AND PASTA

Buffalo Chicken Mac and Cheese

HOT PLATE OR STOVETOP

Serves 2

PREP TIME
5 minutes, plus 15 minutes marinating

COOK TIME
25 minutes

Ingredient Tip: Add some sliced scallion to give this dish a little zing and crunch. Sprinkle the scallion on top just before serving.

The trickiest part of cooking this meal is making the roux—the part where you form a paste out of melted butter and flour, which will thicken the sauce. When you add the milk the sauce may start to get clumpy, but don't worry, keep whisking, gently mashing apart any large clumps, and you'll create a smooth, luscious sauce. Once you stir in the cheese, you'll find yourself scouring your room for anything you can use (Bread? Crackers? Stale cheese puffs?!) to sop up every last drop in your bowl.

FOR THE BUFFALO CHICKEN AND MACARONI

2 boneless, skinless chicken breasts, cut into 1-inch pieces

¼ cup buffalo sauce

Water, for cooking

½ cup dried elbow macaroni

1 tablespoon canola oil

FOR THE CHEESE SAUCE

1 tablespoon unsalted butter

1 tablespoon all-purpose flour

⅔ cup milk

⅔ cup shredded sharp Cheddar cheese

TO MAKE THE BUFFALO CHICKEN AND MACARONI

1. In a shallow bowl, combine the chicken and buffalo sauce, turning the chicken to coat in the sauce. Refrigerate to marinate for at least 15 minutes.
2. Fill a saucepan with water and bring it to a boil over high heat. Add the macaroni and cook until al dente, according to the package instructions. Drain, transfer to a large bowl, and set aside.

3. In a skillet over medium-high heat, warm the canola oil.
4. Using a slotted spoon, transfer the chicken from the bowl to the skillet, leaving behind the sauce, and cook for 4 to 6 minutes, turning halfway through the cooking time, until the chicken is no longer pink when you cut into it with a knife. Remove the chicken from the skillet and add it to the bowl with the pasta.
5. Reduce the heat to medium and return the skillet to the heat. There will be some buffalo sauce in the pan, and that's fine.

TO MAKE THE CHEESE SAUCE

1. Add the butter to the skillet and whisk until melted. Slowly add the flour, whisking until it forms a paste.
2. Gradually whisk in the milk and cook for about 2 minutes until it creates a loose sauce. Stir in the cheese and cook for 2 to 3 minutes until the cheese has melted and the sauce is thick enough to coat the back of a spoon.
3. Pour the cheese sauce over the chicken and macaroni and toss until coated.

PER SERVING: Calories: 692; Total fat: 38g; Carbohydrates: 21g; Fiber: 2g; Protein: 67g

Ramen Alfredo

MICROWAVE

15 MINUTES OR LESS

VEGETARIAN

Serves 2

PREP TIME
5 minutes

COOK TIME
10 minutes

Substitution Tip: No fresh garlic? Use ⅛ teaspoon garlic powder instead.

You can be anything you want to be—just like instant ramen. You don't have to stick to the major you initially declared and you don't need to use that seasoning packet that comes with the ramen, or even follow the instructions on the package. Let this recipe encourage you to mix things up and go with your gut. Literally. This wasn't meant to be a pep talk but, well, here we are. Let this recipe inspire you to follow your dreams and satisfy your craving for Alfredo.

2 (3-ounce) packages instant ramen, noodles only (seasoning packets discarded)

Water, for cooking

4 tablespoons unsalted butter

½ cup heavy (whipping) cream

¼ teaspoon minced garlic

⅛ teaspoon salt

⅛ teaspoon pepper

⅔ cup shredded Parmesan cheese

1. Break the ramen noodles into small pieces and place them in a large microwave-safe bowl. Cover the ramen with water, cover the bowl, and microwave for 3 minutes, or until al dente. Drain and set aside.
2. Place the butter in a small microwave-safe bowl and microwave for 20 seconds, and then in 10-second intervals until melted.

3. Stir in the heavy cream, garlic, salt, and pepper and microwave for 2 to 3 minutes more.
4. Stir in the Parmesan cheese until it melts into the sauce (you may need to microwave it for 30 seconds to help it along). Add the sauce to the noodles and toss to combine.

PER SERVING: Calories: 827; Total fat: 56g; Carbohydrates: 63g; Fiber: 2g; Protein: 20g

Pesto Parm-Stuffed Peppers

MICROWAVE

TOASTER OVEN

5-INGREDIENT

30 MINUTES OR LESS

There will be a night when it feels like the walls are closing in on you and you just want to be far, far away from your dorm—and that essay you need to write and that exam in your 8 a.m. class tomorrow. On that night, make these stuffed peppers. The herby pesto and salty Parmesan are so unlike your typical dining hall fare or any drive-thru meal you'll instantly feel transported to a calmer place. Find prepared pesto at most grocery stores.

Serves 2

PREP TIME
10 minutes

COOK TIME
15 minutes

⅓ cup microwaveable brown rice

2 bell peppers, any color, halved and seeded

¼ cup pesto

2 tablespoons shredded Parmesan cheese, plus more for topping

⅓ cup drained and rinsed canned chickpeas

1. Cook the rice in the microwave according to the package instructions. Drain and set aside.
2. Preheat the toaster oven to broil.
3. Place the bell pepper halves, cut-side up, on the toaster oven tray. Broil for 2 to 3 minutes until tender and charred. Set the temperature to 350°F and remove the peppers from the oven.
4. In a large bowl, stir together the cooked brown rice, pesto, Parmesan cheese, and chickpeas. Spoon the mixture into the pepper halves, sprinkle with additional Parmesan, and bake for 8 to 10 minutes until the cheese melts.

Preparation Tip: Save serious time by making "instant" brown rice instead of the traditional kind. Follow the package instructions and follow the rest of the recipe as instructed.

PER SERVING: Calories: 575; Total fat: 19g; Carbohydrates: 88g; Fiber: 9g; Protein: 14g

Shrimp Scampi with Linguine

Though this dish is typically made with white wine, you won't notice the difference when you combine the butter, chicken broth, and lemon juice. Vegetarians: Swap chicken broth for vegetable broth, keeping in mind some varieties taste really herby, which may affect the flavor of this dish.

HOT PLATE OR STOVETOP

15 MINUTES OR LESS

Serves 2

PREP TIME
5 minutes

COOK TIME
10 minutes

Water, for cooking

¼ (16-ounce) package linguine noodles

8 ounces shrimp, peeled and deveined

Salt

Pepper

3 tablespoons unsalted butter, divided

1 teaspoon minced garlic

¼ cup low-sodium chicken broth

Juice of 1 lemon

1. Fill a saucepan with water and bring it to a boil over high heat. Add the pasta and cook until al dente, according to the package instructions. Drain and set aside.
2. Pat the shrimp dry with a paper towel and season it all over with salt and pepper.
3. In a skillet over medium heat, melt 2 tablespoons of butter.

CONTINUED

Preparation Tip: To devein shrimp, first peel the translucent shell from the shrimp. Run a sharp knife along the back of the shrimp, creating a shallow incision. The vein is the black or gray line running along the back. Using the tip of your knife, pull the vein out of the shrimp.

Shrimp Scampi with Linguine CONTINUED

4. Add the shrimp and cook for about 2 minutes until pink. Transfer the shrimp to a plate and set aside.
5. Return the skillet to the heat and add the garlic and remaining 1 tablespoon of butter. Once the butter melts, stir in the chicken broth and lemon juice and bring the mixture to a boil. Stir the sauce until combined, turn off the heat, add the noodles and shrimp to the skillet, and toss until combined.

PER SERVING: Calories: 397; Total fat: 20g; Carbohydrates: 22g; Fiber: 1g; Protein: 31g

Spaghetti and Mozzarella-Stuffed Meatballs

Gooey cheese takes this classic meal to the next level. If you have a freezer, store the diced cheese there while you prepare the meatballs—it'll help prevent the cheese from oozing out of the meatballs while cooking. (Though, if some does, just scoop the cheese into the pasta. You won't regret it.) Buying a package of string cheese at the grocery store makes it easy to use a little for this recipe and save the rest to snack on later.

MICROWAVE

HOT PLATE OR STOVETOP

TOASTER OVEN

30 MINUTES OR LESS

Serves 2

PREP TIME
5 minutes

COOK TIME
25 minutes

Water, for cooking

½ (16-ounce) package spaghetti

8 ounces ground beef

¼ cup Italian-style bread crumbs

1 large egg

2 sticks mozzarella string cheese, each cut into 4 pieces

2 cups marinara sauce

Salt

Pepper

1. Fill a saucepan with water and bring it to a boil over medium-high heat. Add the spaghetti and cook until al dente, according to the package instructions. Drain and set aside.
2. Preheat the toaster oven to 450°F.
3. In a large bowl, using your clean hands, mix together the ground beef, bread crumbs, and egg until combined. Roll the mixture into 8 meatballs. Using your finger, poke a hole into the center of each meatball. Place 1 piece of mozzarella cheese inside each and mold the meatball around the cheese to close the hole. Place the meatballs on the toaster oven tray.

Substitution Tip: To make this meal gluten free, use ground rolled oats instead of bread crumbs in the meatballs and use chickpea pasta, or cut zucchini into ribbons with a vegetable peeler instead of using the flour-based pasta.

CONTINUED

Spaghetti and Mozzarella-Stuffed Meatballs CONTINUED

4. Bake for 10 to 12 minutes, or until the meat is no longer pink when you cut into it with a knife.
5. Place the marinara in a medium microwave-safe bowl and microwave for 1½ to 2 minutes until hot. Toss the meatballs in the marinara.
6. Divide the pasta between 2 bowls and top with meatballs and marinara. Season with salt and pepper, to taste.

PER SERVING: Calories: 509; Total fat: 26g; Carbohydrates: 27g; Fiber: 4g; Protein: 42g

Chicken Burrito Bowl

If you're craving the flavor of those Tex-Mex chains—you know the ones—but can't bring yourself to shell out the money, you're in luck: It's incredibly easy to create those flavors at home for a fraction of the price. To take it to the next level: Squeeze half a lime over the rice and stir in a pinch of chopped fresh cilantro and let it sit while you prep the rest of the meal.

MICROWAVE

HOT PLATE OR STOVETOP

30 MINUTES OR LESS

Serves 1

PREP TIME
10 minutes

COOK TIME
10 minutes

¼ cup microwaveable white rice, or brown rice

1 boneless, skinless chicken breast, cut into bite-size pieces

1 teaspoon chili powder

1 tablespoon vegetable oil

½ (15-ounce) can black beans, drained and rinsed

½ cup shredded lettuce

1 tablespoon shredded Mexican-style cheese blend

¼ cup salsa

1. Cook the rice in the microwave according to the package instructions.
2. Pat the chicken dry with a paper towel and season both sides with chili powder.
3. In a skillet over medium-high heat, warm the vegetable oil.
4. Add the chicken and cook for 4 to 6 minutes, turning halfway through the cooking time, until the chicken is no longer pink when you cut into it with a knife.

Substitution Tip: To make this a vegan bowl, skip the chicken and the cheese (or use a nut-based cheese alternative) and scatter in some diced avocado or diced roasted sweet potato.

CONTINUED

Chicken Burrito Bowl CONTINUED

5. Place the black beans in a small microwave-safe bowl and microwave for about 2 minutes until hot.
6. In a medium bowl, stir together the rice, warmed beans, and chicken. Top with the lettuce, cheese, and salsa.

PER SERVING: Calories: 464; Total fat: 7g; Carbohydrates: 66g; Fiber: 13g; Protein: 37g

Budget Pad Thai

You won't find peanut butter in authentic pad thai—that flavor usually comes from crushed peanuts—but it's one of the best shortcuts to getting that umami (savory) flavor without having to buy fish sauce and tamarind paste. The peanut butter paired with lime juice, brown sugar, and soy sauce, creates that salty, tangy, sweet flavor combo that will have you craving this at any hour of the day.

MICROWAVE

HOT PLATE OR STOVETOP

15 MINUTES OR LESS

VEGETARIAN

Serves 2

PREP TIME
5 minutes

COOK TIME
10 minutes

Ingredient Tip: If you like a little heat, drizzle the pad thai with sriracha. An extra squeeze of lime juice will also unlock a whole new layer of flavor.

FOR THE THAI SAUCE

Juice of 1 lime

2 tablespoons light brown sugar

2 tablespoons low-sodium soy sauce

2 tablespoons creamy peanut butter

FOR THE NOODLES

Water, for cooking

4 ounces wide rice noodles

2 large eggs

¼ teaspoon low-sodium soy sauce

Salt

Pepper

1 tablespoon sliced scallion (green part only)

TO MAKE THE THAI SAUCE

In a small bowl, whisk the lime juice, brown sugar, soy sauce, and peanut butter and set aside.

CONTINUED

Budget Pad Thai CONTINUED

TO MAKE THE NOODLES

1. Fill a medium saucepan with water and bring it to a boil over medium-high heat. Add the rice noodles and cook according to the package instructions. Drain, return the noodles to the saucepan, and set aside.
2. Crack the eggs into a microwave-safe bowl, add the soy sauce, and season with salt and pepper. Lightly whisk to combine. Microwave for 45 seconds, stir, and microwave in 25-second intervals until the eggs are lightly scrambled. Break up the eggs with a spoon and add them to the pan with the noodles.
3. Add the Thai sauce to the noodles and eggs, stirring to combine. Divide the mixture between 2 bowls and top with sliced scallion.

MAKE IT GLUTEN FREE: Use tamari, which is not made with wheat, in place of soy sauce and always remember to check packaging ingredients to ensure foods, especially oats, were processed in a completely gluten-free facility.

PER SERVING: Calories: 283; Total fat: 14g; Carbohydrates: 30g; Fiber: 2g; Protein: 12g

Beef and Broccoli Ramen

"You made that? You didn't order it?" That was the most common reaction people had when I Instagrammed this dish, which is the same reaction everyone around you will have when they smell this sweet, garlicky sauce wafting down the hall. Don't be surprised if people ask you to share.

MICROWAVE

HOT PLATE OR STOVETOP

30 MINUTES OR LESS

Serves 2

PREP TIME
10 minutes, plus 10 minutes marinating

COOK TIME
15 minutes

½ cup low-sodium soy sauce, divided

Juice of 2 limes, divided

4 tablespoons packed light brown sugar, divided

8 ounces sirloin steak, cut into thin slices

1 tablespoon vegetable oil, or canola oil

2 (3-ounce) packages instant ramen, noodles only (seasoning packets discarded)

Water, for cooking

½ teaspoon garlic powder

½ head broccoli, cut into florets

1. In a large bowl, stir together ¼ cup of soy sauce, half the lime juice, and 2 tablespoons of brown sugar. Add the steak, tossing to coat, and set aside to marinate for 10 minutes.
2. In a large skillet over medium heat, warm the vegetable oil.
3. Remove the meat from the marinade and discard the marinade. Add the marinated meat to the skillet and cook for 2 to 3 minutes per side until browned. Transfer the steak to a plate and set aside.

Preparation Tip: To make the steak easy to cut, freeze it for 10 minutes before cutting and it will be easy to get perfectly thin slices. Set a timer so you won't forget it's in there and freezes solid.

CONTINUED

Beef and Broccoli Ramen CONTINUED

4. Place the ramen noodles in a large microwave-safe bowl, cover with water, and top with a microwave-safe plate. Microwave for 2½ to 3 minutes, or until the noodles are tender. Drain and set aside.
5. Return the skillet to medium-high heat and add the remaining ¼ cup of soy sauce, remaining lime juice, remaining 2 tablespoons of brown sugar, and the garlic powder, stirring to combine. Add the broccoli, bring the mixture to a simmer, and cook for about 5 minutes, stirring occasionally, or until cooked through.
6. Divide the noodles between 2 bowls. Top with the beef and broccoli and toss to coat the noodles in the sauce.

PER SERVING: Calories: 744; Total fat: 15g; Carbohydrates: 103g; Fiber: 11g; Protein: 57g

Ridiculously Easy Fried Rice

A splash of sesame oil—also used in the Easy Beef Bibimbap (page 103)—mixed into the fried rice at the end will give this dish that slightly toasted flavor you're familiar with. However, if you don't think you'll use the oil often, make this dish without and it will still be plenty tasty.

MICROWAVE

30 MINUTES OR LESS

Serves 1

PREP TIME
5 minutes

COOK TIME
15 minutes

- **⅓ cup microwaveable white rice, or brown rice**
- **¼ onion, chopped**
- **¼ cup frozen peas and carrots**
- **1 teaspoon vegetable oil**
- **1 large egg**
- **¼ cup diced cooked ham, or cooked, crumbled bacon**
- **2 teaspoons low-sodium soy sauce**

1. Cook the rice in the microwave according to the package instructions. Set aside.
2. In a medium microwave-safe bowl, stir together the onion, peas and carrots, and vegetable oil. Microwave for 45 seconds, or until the onion is translucent.
3. In a small microwave-safe bowl, lightly whisk the egg. Microwave it for 40 seconds, stir, and microwave in 20-second intervals until the egg has set. Use a spoon to break up the egg into small, bite-size pieces. Add the egg to the cooked vegetables, along with the cooked rice, ham, and soy sauce. Toss to combine.

Preparation Tip: Make a big batch of rice over the weekend and refrigerate it in an airtight container. To reheat, place 1 cup of rice in a microwave-safe bowl with 2 tablespoons of water. Cover with a paper towel and cook for about 1 minute, or until the rice has warmed through. Drain any excess water before mixing it with the rest of the ingredients.

CONTINUED

Ridiculously Easy Fried Rice CONTINUED

MAKE IT GLUTEN FREE: Use tamari, which is not made with wheat, in place of soy sauce and always remember to check packaging ingredients to ensure foods, especially oats, were processed in a completely gluten-free facility.

PER SERVING: Calories: 439; Total fat: 13g; Carbohydrates: 57g; Fiber: 4g; Protein: 22g

Easy Beef Bibimbap

Pronounced "bee-beem-bap," this Korean dish is as versatile as the name is fun to say. (Admit it: You've already said it in your head three times fast.) It's typically a mix of rice and veggies, but you can add a fried egg or other protein to make it more filling.

MICROWAVE

HOT PLATE OR STOVETOP

30 MINUTES OR LESS

Serves 2

PREP TIME
10 minutes

COOK TIME
20 minutes

Substitution Tip: Traditionally, bibimbap recipes call for gochujang, a Korean pepper paste, so use that if you can find it, but sriracha, which can be easier to find, is just as tasty.

FOR THE RICE

⅔ cup microwaveable jasmine rice

FOR THE BIBIMBAP SAUCE

2 tablespoons low-sodium soy sauce

1 tablespoon sesame oil

1 tablespoon rice vinegar (optional)

1 tablespoon sugar

2 teaspoons sriracha

FOR THE BEEF AND VEGETABLES

1 large carrot

1 tablespoon olive oil

1 zucchini, end trimmed, halved lengthwise, thinly sliced into half-moons

8 ounces ground beef

1 teaspoon minced garlic

2 tablespoons sliced scallion

TO MAKE THE RICE

Cook the rice in the microwave according to the package instructions and set aside.

CONTINUED

Easy Beef Bibimbap CONTINUED

TO MAKE THE BIBIMBAP SAUCE

In a small bowl, stir together the soy sauce, sesame oil, vinegar (if using), sugar, and sriracha. Set aside.

TO MAKE THE BEEF AND VEGETABLES

1. Using a vegetable peeler, peel the carrot into long ribbons.
2. In a skillet over medium heat, warm the olive oil.
3. Add the zucchini and carrot and cook for 4 to 5 minutes until tender. Transfer the vegetables to a plate and set aside.
4. Return the skillet to the heat and add the ground beef and garlic. Cook for 3 to 4 minutes, breaking up the meat with a wooden spoon, until it's no longer pink. Turn off the heat. Add the zucchini and carrots, scallion, and bibimbap sauce. Stir, coating everything in the sauce.
5. Divide the rice between 2 bowls and top with the meat and vegetable mixture.

MAKE IT GLUTEN FREE: Use tamari, which is not made with wheat, in place of soy sauce and always remember to check packaging ingredients to ensure foods, especially oats, were processed in a completely gluten-free facility.

PER SERVING: Calories: 504; Total fat: 26g; Carbohydrates: 32g; Fiber: 3g; Protein: 34g

TOASTER OVEN CHICKEN AND VEGETABLES
(PAGE 116)

chapter 8

HEARTY MAINS

Greek Flatbread

NO COOK

30 MINUTES OR LESS

ONE BOWL

VEGAN

Serves 1

PREP TIME
10 minutes, plus 15 minutes marinating

Preparation Tip: Take this meal to the next level by toasting the pita before adding the toppings, and sprinkling chopped fresh dill and feta cheese over the whole thing before serving.

This is the perfect fried food—as in, the perfect food to make when it's been a crazy long day, your brain is fried, and you want to eat something good right now that you could practically whip up in your sleep. Keep these ingredients on hand and you'll be able to make this in a snap.

½ cucumber, chopped

¼ cup Kalamata olives, pitted and halved

¼ cup grape tomatoes, halved

2 teaspoons olive oil

1 teaspoon freshly squeezed lemon juice

⅛ teaspoon salt

1 (6½-inch) pita bread

2 tablespoons garlic hummus

1. In a medium bowl, stir together the cucumber, olives, tomatoes, olive oil, lemon juice, and salt. Set aside for 15 minutes to marinate.
2. Place the pita on a work surface. Spread the hummus over the pita. Top with the vegetable mixture, relax, and eat.

PER SERVING: Calories: 515; Total fat: 32g; Carbohydrates: 49g; Fiber: 5g; Protein: 9g

Loaded Veggie Frittata

When you're in the mood for something fast, easy, and pretty healthy, look no further. This simple frittata is great for days when your schedule is packed and you're craving a warm meal to scarf between evening classes. Stirring milk into the egg mixture produces a fluffy frittata; if you don't have milk on hand, omit it.

MICROWAVE

15 MINUTES OR LESS

VEGETARIAN

Serves 1

PREP TIME
10 minutes

COOK TIME
3 minutes

1 tablespoon diced button mushrooms

1 tablespoon diced bell pepper, any color

2 teaspoons diced white onion

¼ teaspoon olive oil

2 large eggs, lightly whisked

1 teaspoon milk

1 tablespoon crumbled feta cheese

Salt

Pepper

1. In a medium microwave-safe bowl, stir together the mushrooms, bell pepper, onion, and olive oil. Microwave for 45 to 55 seconds, or until the onion is translucent. Drain any excess liquid.
2. Add the eggs, milk, and feta cheese and stir to combine. Season with salt and pepper, to taste. Microwave for 1½ minutes. Use a fork to break up the eggs and push the runny center toward the edges. Microwave for 30 to 40 seconds more, or until the eggs are no longer runny. Pausing halfway through to stir the egg mixture is crucial because microwaves cook food from the outside in; the eggs will get rubbery on the outside and remain soft on the inside if you don't.

Ingredient Tip: This is a great clear-out-your-fridge meal. As long as you have eggs, salt, and pepper, you can change out which vegetables and cheese you mix in. I try to stick to 2 or 3 mix-ins, just to vary the texture and flavor of each bite.

PER SERVING: Calories: 221; Total fat: 13g; Carbohydrates: 8g; Fiber: 2g; Protein: 16g

Hot Wings and Sweet Potato Fries

MICROWAVE

TOASTER OVEN

Serves 1

PREP TIME
15 minutes

COOK TIME
1 hour, 10 minutes

Preparation Tip: If you can only find whole chicken wings, cut them diagonally through their joint. Cut off and discard the wing tips.

These wings rival any you'd find at a restaurant and they get just as crispy as the fried kind, without all the grease. The keys to success are tossing the chicken with baking powder, the long bake time, and the broil at the end. These wings are worth the wait.

FOR THE HOT WINGS

8 ounces chicken wingettes and drumettes

Salt

Pepper

½ teaspoon baking powder

Vegetable oil, for cooking

2 tablespoons unsalted butter

3 tablespoons hot sauce

FOR THE SWEET POTATO FRIES

½ sweet potato, peeled and cut into fries

1 teaspoon vegetable oil

Salt

TO MAKE THE HOT WINGS

1. Preheat the toaster oven to 450°F.
2. Pat the chicken dry with a paper towel and season both sides with salt and pepper. In a medium bowl, toss the chicken with the baking powder to lightly coat.
3. Add some vegetable oil to a paper towel and rub it on the wire rack of the toaster oven. Place the wings on the rack and place the toaster oven tray directly below the wings to catch any fat drips.

4. Bake for 30 to 35 minutes, or until the chicken has browned and is no longer pink when you cut into it with a knife.
5. Set the toaster oven to broil and cook for 2 to 3 minutes more, or until the skin is crispy. Transfer the wings to a large bowl and set aside.
6. Reduce the toaster oven temperature to 400°F.
7. Place the butter in a small microwave-safe bowl and microwave for 25 seconds. Stir, and microwave another 10 to 20 seconds more, or until the butter is completely melted. Stir in the hot sauce. Add the hot sauce mixture to the wings and toss to coat.

TO MAKE THE SWEET POTATO FRIES

1. With oven mitts on, wipe the toaster oven tray clean with a paper towel.
2. In a large bowl, toss together the sweet potatoes, vegetable oil, and salt to coat. Spread the potatoes on the toaster oven tray in a single layer.
3. Bake 20 minutes, or until the edges have browned.

MAKE IT GLUTEN FREE: Double-check that your baking powder is made with cornstarch or potato starch (most brands in the United States are) and always remember to check packaging ingredients to ensure foods, especially oats, were processed in a completely gluten-free facility.

PER SERVING: Calories: 381; Total fat: 32g; Carbohydrates: 7g; Fiber: 1g; Protein: 17g

Chili Loaded Sweet Potatoes

MICROWAVE

HOT PLATE OR STOVETOP

Serves 2

PREP TIME
10 minutes

COOK TIME
20 minutes

Ingredient Tip: To take the heat level down a notch, seed the jalapeno before dicing it.

Preparation Tip: You can easily double the recipe and refrigerate the chili in a large airtight container, giving you enough for a week of lunches.

This is the perfect meal for a chilly fall night—hearty and satisfying—yet, with ground turkey and sweet potatoes, it won't send you into a food coma right after you eat it. If you like a little more heat, add a pinch of cayenne pepper or a drizzle of your favorite hot sauce. You'll be surprised how the sweet potatoes soothe the kick so you get the flavor without the lingering burn.

2 sweet potatoes

8 ounces ground turkey

1 teaspoon chili powder

½ white onion, diced

1 (15-ounce) can kidney beans, drained and rinsed

1 (14.5-ounce) can fire-roasted tomatoes, drained

1 teaspoon diced seeded jalapeño pepper

2 tablespoons shredded sharp Cheddar cheese

1. Pierce the sweet potatoes all over with a fork. Wrap them in a damp paper towel and microwave until tender, 4 to 5 minutes.
2. In a saucepan over medium heat, combine the ground turkey, chili powder, and onion. Cook for 3 to 4 minutes, breaking up the meat with a spoon, until browned. Drain any excess grease.
3. Stir in the kidney beans, tomatoes, and jalapeño and bring the mixture to a simmer. Cook, stirring occasionally, for 10 minutes.

4. Halve the sweet potatoes almost all the way through. Spoon the chili over the sweet potatoes and top with the Cheddar cheese.

MAKE IT GLUTEN FREE: Check the label on the chili powder to make sure it doesn't use wheat flour as a filler and always remember to check packaging ingredients to ensure foods, especially oats, were processed in a completely gluten-free facility.

PER SERVING: Calories: 614; Total fat: 21g; Carbohydrates: 68; Fiber: 16g; Protein: 40g

Philly Cheesesteak Baked Potatoes

MICROWAVE

HOT PLATE OR STOVETOP

Serves 2

PREP TIME
10 minutes

COOK TIME
20 minutes, plus cooling

Substitution Tip: If you can't find provolone, go with one of the other two cheesesteak standbys: slices of American cheese or a squirt of canned cheese.

Fans of this classic sandwich love to debate what constitutes the best cheesesteak. It's pretty much agreed upon that you need to cut the steak as thinly as possible and the best way to do that is to freeze it for a few minutes beforehand, which will make it easier to cut into those paper-thin slices. Some combination of peppers, onions, and cheese is also a must. This cheesesteak has all that but, instead of a hoagie roll, I spoon it over a baked potato.

- **2 russet potatoes**
- **2 tablespoons sour cream (optional)**
- **2 teaspoons olive oil**
- **1 bell pepper, any color, seeded and cut into slices**
- **1 yellow onion, cut into slices**
- **1 (8-ounce) flank steak or pepper steak, very thinly sliced**
- **¼ teaspoon salt**
- **¼ teaspoon pepper**
- **4 slices provolone cheese**

1. Pierce the potatoes all over with a fork, wrap them in a damp paper towel, and microwave for 5 minutes, or until tender. When cool, halve them almost all the way through and dollop with sour cream (if using).
2. In a skillet over medium heat, warm the olive oil. Add the bell pepper and onion and cook for 5 to 7 minutes until the onion is tender and lightly golden.

3. Season the steak with salt and pepper and add it to the skillet with the vegetables. Cook for 2 to 4 minutes, stirring occasionally, until the steak is browned and no longer pink or translucent when you cut into it with a knife.
4. Spoon the steak, bell pepper, and onion over the potatoes and top each with 2 slices of provolone cheese.

PER SERVING: Calories: 600; Total fat: 21g; Carbohydrates: 51g; Fiber: 7g; Protein: 51g

Toaster Oven Chicken and Vegetables

TOASTER OVEN

Serves 1

PREP TIME
5 minutes, plus 20 minutes marinating

COOK TIME
25 minutes

Substitution Tip: If you don't have time to marinate the chicken, no worries, simply skip that step and season the chicken with salt and pepper (or the leftover ranch seasoning from the Zesty Ranch Potato Tots on page 41) and prepare the recipe as instructed.

Sheet pan dinners have become a hit on Pinterest, and for good reason: You can cook a whole meal and dirty just one pan, which cuts down on the work considerably. This version has been scaled down to fit in your toaster oven. If you have an extra-small appliance, you can always cook the vegetables first and reheat them in the microwave once the chicken is ready.

1 boneless, skinless chicken breast

¼ cup Italian dressing

3 baby red potatoes, quartered

1 tablespoon olive oil, divided

1 teaspoon garlic powder, divided

Salt

½ cup green beans, trimmed

1. Place the chicken in a shallow bowl, cover with the Italian dressing, and refrigerate to marinate for at least 20 minutes.
2. Preheat the toaster oven to 400°F.
3. In a medium bowl, stir together the potatoes, 1½ teaspoons of olive oil, and ½ teaspoon of garlic powder. Season with salt, to taste, and toss until the potatoes are coated. Place the potatoes on one side of the toaster oven tray in a single layer, leaving room in the center.
4. Remove the chicken from the marinade, shake off any excess dressing, and place it in the center of the toaster oven tray.

5. Bake for 15 minutes.
6. In the small bowl, toss the green beans with the remaining 1½ teaspoons of olive oil and the remaining ½ teaspoon of garlic powder. Season with salt, to taste, and add the green beans to the tray.
7. Bake for 10 minutes more, or until the green beans are tender and the chicken is no longer pink when you cut into it with a knife.

PER SERVING: Calories: 744; Total fat: 28g; Carbohydrates: 91g; Fiber: 8g; Protein: 36g

Eggplant Mozzarella

HOT PLATE OR STOVETOP

TOASTER OVEN

VEGETARIAN

Serves 2

PREP TIME
15 minutes

COOK TIME
35 minutes

Preparation Tip: The cooking spray ensures that the bread crumbs will be golden and crispy, as though you fried the eggplant. If you don't have cooking spray, lightly brush the eggplant with vegetable oil.

You'll want to bust out a tablecloth and put some flowers in a vase—if you have those things—when you prepare this dish. It's everything you'd expect from a restaurant, served right in your room.

Water, for cooking

½ (16-ounce) package pasta of choice

1 small eggplant, peeled and cut into ¼-inch-thick slices

1 large egg

⅓ cup milk

1 cup Italian-style bread crumbs

Nonstick cooking spray

4 cups marinara sauce, plus more as needed

½ cup shredded mozzarella cheese

Salt

Pepper

1. Fill a saucepan with water and bring it to a boil over high heat. Cook the pasta al dente according to the package directions. Drain and set aside.
2. Pat the eggplant dry with a paper towel.
3. Preheat the toaster oven to 375°F.
4. Crack the egg into a shallow bowl, add the milk, and beat the mixture with a fork until combined. Place the bread crumbs on a plate or in another shallow bowl and position it next to the egg mixture. Using a fork or tongs, dip 1 eggplant slice into the egg mixture, coating it entirely and shaking off any excess. Dip the slice into the bread crumbs, turning it so both sides are coated, and set it aside on a plate. Repeat with the remaining eggplant slices.

5. Spray the toaster oven tray with cooking spray. Position as many eggplant slices as you can fit in a single layer on the tray. (You may need to cook the eggplant in batches, depending on the size of your oven.) Spray the top of the eggplant with more cooking spray.
6. Bake for 15 to 17 minutes, or until the bread crumbs are lightly golden. Spoon marinara over the top and around the eggplant, top with mozzarella cheese, and bake for 5 to 7 minutes more, or until the cheese has melted.
7. Divide the pasta between 2 bowls and top with the eggplant and additional marinara, if desired.

PER SERVING: Calories: 746; Total fat: 18g; Carbohydrates: 125g; Fiber: 19g; Protein: 30g

Vegetarian Burrito Boat

TOASTER OVEN

5-INGREDIENT

30 MINUTES OR LESS

VEGETARIAN

Serves 1

PREP TIME
5 minutes

COOK TIME
20 minutes

Preparation Tip: If you're cooking for your roommates—quadruple this recipe and bake it in the oven at the same temperature and for the same amount of time.

Anyone who says meatless meals lack flavor needs to try this dish. It takes minutes to make and will satisfy even the most hardcore carnivores in your crew.

1 zucchini, ends trimmed, halved lengthwise

3 tablespoons salsa

¼ cup drained and rinsed canned black beans

⅛ teaspoon salt

1 tablespoon shredded Mexican-style cheese blend

1. Preheat the toaster oven to 350°F.
2. Using a spoon, scoop out the seedy pulp from the zucchini halves, forming a well. Finely chop the pulp and place it in a small bowl. Stir in the salsa, beans, and salt.
3. Place the zucchini halves, cut-side up, in a small, oven-safe casserole dish. Fill each zucchini with the salsa mixture and top with shredded cheese.
4. Bake for 15 to 20 minutes, or until the zucchini is tender and the cheese has melted.

MAKE IT VEGAN: Omit the shredded cheese, or try a dairy-free blend, such as Daiya®.

PER SERVING: Calories: 155; Total fat: 4g Carbohydrates: 25g; Fiber: 9g; Protein: 10g

Veggie Fajitas

You don't need meat to enjoy fajitas. The key to this recipe is to make sure the pan is nice and hot, letting the onions caramelize a little as they cook, and taking the veggies off the heat while they still have a little snap to them.

HOT PLATE OR STOVETOP

30 MINUTES OR LESS

VEGAN

Serves 2

PREP TIME
10 minutes

COOK TIME
8 minutes

2 teaspoons vegetable oil

1 bell pepper, any color, seeded and cut into slices

½ onion, cut into slices

4 to 5 button mushrooms, cut into slices

½ teaspoon minced garlic

Salt

Pepper

2 small flour tortillas

Juice of ¼ lime

1. In a skillet over medium-high heat, warm the vegetable oil.
2. Add the bell pepper and onion and sauté for about 2 minutes until the onion is translucent.
3. Add the mushrooms and garlic and sauté for about 5 minutes until the mushrooms are tender. Season with salt and pepper, to taste.
4. Place the tortillas on a work surface. Pile the vegetables onto the tortillas. Drizzle with lime juice and serve.

MAKE IT GLUTEN FREE: Use corn tortillas instead of flour tortillas and always remember to check packaging ingredients to ensure foods, especially oats, were processed in a completely gluten-free facility.

PER SERVING: Calories: 522; Total fat: 17g; Carbohydrates: 77g; Fiber: 8g; Protein: 14g

Substitution Tip: Not everyone likes mushrooms, so, if that's you, try this with black beans instead. Or add sliced avocado. If you eat meat, add some cut-up leftover chicken from Toaster Oven Chicken and Vegetables (page 116).

Microwave Tamale Pie

MICROWAVE

30 MINUTES OR LESS

Serves 4

PREP TIME
5 minutes

COOK TIME
20 minutes

Ingredient Tip: Make sure you have the ingredients necessary to make the corn bread batter, which usually include an egg and some milk. I like Jiffy® brand corn bread mix but use whichever you like.

If you're having friends over and you really want to impress, this recipe will do it. It's hearty, loaded with flavor, and almost impossible to believe it's made entirely in the microwave. And, if you have leftovers, they reheat well, too.

1 (8.5-ounce) box instant corn bread mix, such as Jiffy® (plus any ingredients the package requires)

1 pound ground beef

1 teaspoon chili powder

Salt

Pepper

1 (16-ounce) can corn, drained

⅔ cup picante sauce, or chunky salsa, plus more for topping

¼ cup shredded Mexican-style cheese blend

1. In a medium bowl, stir together the corn bread batter following the package instructions and set aside.
2. In a medium microwave-safe casserole dish, stir together the ground beef and chili powder and season with salt and pepper, to taste, breaking up the meat with the spoon. Stir in the corn and picante sauce and stir until combined. Spread the mixture into the dish, using the spoon to form a well in the middle (this will help the meat cook more evenly).
3. Microwave for 5 minutes, stir the meat, breaking it up into crumbles, and microwave for 6 minutes more, or until the beef is no longer pink. Drain any excess juices.

4. Spoon a thin layer of corn bread batter over the meat mixture in the casserole dish. Microwave at 70 percent power for 5 minutes.
5. Sprinkle the cheese over the top and microwave at 70 percent power for 2 minutes more, or until the cheese has melted and a toothpick inserted into the corn bread comes out clean. Serve with additional picante sauce for topping.

PER SERVING: Calories: 623; Total fat: 30g; Carbohydrates: 50g; Fiber: 6g; Protein: 40g

Date Night Steak and Mashed Potatoes

HOT PLATE OR STOVETOP

30 MINUTES OR LESS

Serves 2

PREP TIME
7 minutes

COOK TIME
25 minutes, plus a few minutes resting

Substitution Tip: You can use butter instead of oil to cook the steaks (some people prefer the flavor), but avoid using olive oil here. It starts to smoke at a lower temperature—around 325°F—which could trigger your fire alarm.

Perfectly searing a steak isn't a requirement to get your degree, but it should be. Most first-timers overcook the steak, which then ends up chewy, bland, and a woeful shade of gray. What they don't realize is they need to get the pan nice and hot before adding the steaks to it. It sparks what's known as the Maillard reaction, where the sugars and amino acids in the meat start to brown, giving the steak a nice crust and its irresistible savory flavor. Once you master this technique, perfectly seared chicken, pork, fish, you name it, will be part of your repertoire.

5 or 6 Yukon gold potatoes, or red potatoes, peeled and quartered

Water, for cooking

¼ cup milk

2 teaspoons garlic powder, divided

2 tablespoons unsalted butter

Salt

Pepper

2 (8-ounce) sirloin steaks

1 tablespoon vegetable oil

1. Place the potatoes in a medium saucepan, cover them with water, and bring to a boil over high heat. Reduce the heat to medium and cook the potatoes for 15 minutes until tender when pierced with a fork. Drain and return the potatoes to the pot.
2. Using a potato masher or a large fork, slightly mash the potatoes. Add the milk, 1½ teaspoons of garlic powder, and the butter, mashing and mixing to combine. Season with salt and pepper, to taste. Cover to keep warm and set aside.

3. Heat a skillet over medium-high heat.
4. Pat the steaks dry with a paper towel and season both sides with salt and pepper, to taste, and the remaining ½ teaspoon of garlic powder.
5. Add the vegetable oil to the skillet. If the skillet is hot enough the oil should sizzle a little. If it doesn't sizzle, it's a sign the skillet isn't hot enough. Wait 30 seconds to 1 minute, watching the oil until its surface starts to shimmer, then add the steaks. Cook the steaks, without moving them, for 4 to 5 minutes. Using a spatula, flip the steaks and cook for 2 to 3 minutes more until the edges turn brown. To test for doneness for a medium steak, press the meat with a pair of tongs—it should be as tender as pressing your finger to your chin. Transfer the steaks to a cutting board to rest for a few minutes.
6. Place each steak on a plate and add a spoonful of mashed potatoes on the side.

PER SERVING: Calories: 624; Total fat: 23g; Carbohydrates: 71g; Fiber: 7g; Protein: 35g

Teriyaki Tofu and Broccoli

TOASTER OVEN

VEGAN

Serves 2

PREP TIME
5 minutes, plus 10 minutes draining

COOK TIME
35 minutes

If it's your first time working with tofu, it's pretty easy—and surprisingly satisfying—to cook with, especially when you let your toaster oven do all the work. A little cornstarch really helps the tofu get a little crust to the edges, so it has a satisfying chewy texture. This dish tastes great on its own or served on a bed of rice.

1 (16-ounce) package extra-firm tofu, drained

⅓ cup, plus 2 tablespoons teriyaki sauce

1 head broccoli, cut into florets

2 teaspoons garlic powder, divided

2 tablespoons cornstarch

Nonstick cooking spray

1. Wrap the tofu between layers of paper towel or in a clean kitchen towel and set a weight on top to remove as much liquid as possible. Let sit for at least 10 minutes, replacing the paper towel as needed.
2. Preheat the toaster oven to 425°F.
3. Cut the tofu into bite-size cubes and place them in a medium bowl. Add 2 tablespoons of teriyaki sauce and toss the tofu to coat.
4. In another medium bowl, toss the broccoli with 1 teaspoon of garlic powder. Spread in an even layer on the toaster oven tray.
5. Bake for 15 minutes, or until the edges of the broccoli are lightly charred. Transfer to a bowl and set aside. Wipe the tray clean with a paper towel.

6. Drain any excess liquid from the tofu. Add the cornstarch and the remaining 1 teaspoon of garlic powder and toss to coat.
7. Spray the toaster oven tray with cooking spray. Spread the tofu in a single layer on the tray.
8. Bake 15 to 17 minutes, or until the edges are lightly golden.
9. Add the tofu to the bowl with the broccoli. Add the remaining ⅓ cup teriyaki sauce and toss to coat.

PER SERVING: Calories: 392; Total fat: 13g; Carbohydrates: 43g; Fiber: 9g; Protein: 36g

TOASTER OVEN S'MORES
(PAGE 133)

chapter 9

DESSERTS

Banana Pudding

NO COOK

5-INGREDIENT

15 MINUTES OR LESS

VEGETARIAN

Serves 2

PREP TIME
15 minutes

Substitution Tip: There is no shame in using store-bought whipped cream or topping. If you use frozen, let it thaw for a bit so it's easy to fold the pudding into.

The best banana pudding has a light, fluffy, almost mousse-like, texture and there's a secret to getting it just so: You fold the pudding into the whipped cream. You can easily make your own, even if you don't have an electric hand mixer—you just need a jar with a lid. Make sure the cream's nice and cold; it'll help the whipped cream fluff up. (While you're at it, don't be confined to vanilla pudding. Chocolate is delicious, too.)

⅓ cup cold heavy (whipping) cream

¼ teaspoon sugar

2 (3.25-ounce) containers vanilla pudding

1 banana, peeled and cut into slices

10 vanilla wafer cookies

1. In a medium airtight container, combine the heavy cream and sugar. Seal the lid and shake vigorously for 3 to 4 minutes, or until the mixture has thickened to create a soft whipped cream. Alternatively, if you have an electric hand mixer, put the ingredients into a medium bowl and beat until soft peaks form, 2 to 3 minutes.
2. Gently fold in the vanilla pudding. Pour one-third of the mixture into a medium bowl.
3. Top with a layer of banana slices and a layer of wafer cookies.
4. Repeat: pudding, banana slices, wafer cookies, and top with the remaining pudding.

PER SERVING: Calories: 378; Total fat: 21g; Carbohydrates: 47g; Fiber: 2g; Protein: 4g

Ice Cream Sandwich Cake

When you make this everybody will freak out, wondering how on earth you made an ice cream cake in your dorm—but, honestly, it couldn't be easier. If you don't have an electric hand mixer to make the whipped cream, you can buy the frozen kind, letting it thaw just enough so it's spreadable, and mix in the cocoa powder.

NO COOK

5-INGREDIENT

VEGETARIAN

Serves 6

PREP TIME
15 minutes, plus 4 hours freezing

1 cup heavy (whipping) cream

1 tablespoon sugar

2 tablespoons unsweetened cocoa powder

6 chocolate sandwich cookies, crumbled

1 (8-pack) box ice cream sandwiches

1. In a large bowl, stir together the heavy cream, sugar, and cocoa powder. Using an electric hand mixer, beat the mixture for about 3 minutes until it forms stiff peaks. Fold in half the crumbled cookie pieces and set aside.
2. Unwrap 4 of the ice cream sandwiches and place them in a 9-by-5-inch loaf pan. Spread half the whipped cream mixture on top in an even layer. Add another layer of 4 ice cream sandwiches and cover with the remaining whipped cream. Sprinkle with the remaining crumbled cookies. Freeze until set, at least 4 hours.

PER SERVING: Calories: 520; Total fat: 29g; Carbohydrates: 60g; Fiber: 2g; Protein: 6g

Substitution Tip: If you're not into a lot of chocolate, omit the cocoa powder. Or cut out the whipped cream layer entirely and spread thawed ice cream in your choice of flavor over the ice cream sandwiches. It will take longer to freeze completely.

Triple Chocolate No-Churn Ice Cream

NO COOK

5-INGREDIENT

VEGETARIAN

Serves 8

PREP TIME
10 minutes, plus 2 hours freezing

Preparation Tip: If you don't want to wait 2 hours for ice cream, pour the mixture into a wider, shallower bowl (one that will fit in your freezer). The increased surface area will reduce the time it takes the dessert to harden.

Yes, you can make ice cream without an ice cream machine. And without having to fuss with cooking eggs in a hot water bath. This frozen treat's as creamy as gelato and as satisfying as anything you'd buy at your favorite scoop shop.

- **2 cups heavy (whipping) cream**
- **1 can sweetened condensed milk**
- **½ cup cocoa powder**
- **⅔ cup semisweet chocolate chips**
- **¼ cup hot fudge sauce**

1. Pour the heavy cream into a large bowl and, using an electric hand mixer, whip the cream for 2 to 3 minutes until stiff peaks form. Add the sweetened condensed milk and cocoa powder and beat until thoroughly combined.
2. Using a spatula, fold in the chocolate chips and half the fudge sauce. Pour the mixture into a 9-by-5-inch loaf pan and top with the remaining fudge sauce. Freeze for at least 2 hours, or overnight. Scoop and serve.

PER SERVING: Calories: 456; Total fat: 28g; Carbohydrates: 51g; Fiber: 3g; Protein: 8g

Toaster Oven S'mores

Yes, you absolutely can enjoy this campfire classic even when you're miles away from the nearest KOA. The trick is to put the toaster oven tray on its lowest rack and to place the marshmallows on their side—if you need to—to make sure they don't puff up and hit the top of the oven. They'll toast quickly on broil, so keep an eye on them, unless you like yours charred to a crisp.

TOASTER OVEN

5-INGREDIENT

15 MINUTES OR LESS

VEGETARIAN

Serves 2

PREP TIME
5 minutes

COOK TIME
1 minute

2 graham cracker sheets, broken in half

1 chocolate bar, broken in half

2 jumbo marshmallows

1. Place 2 graham crackers halves on the toaster oven tray. Top each with a piece of chocolate. Turn the marshmallows on their sides and place them on the chocolate, so the marshmallows appear short and wide, not tall (If there is a top rack you can remove, take it out.)
2. Set the toaster oven to broil. Bake the s'mores for 30 to 45 seconds until the marshmallows are puffy and lightly golden. Remove them from the toaster oven and top with the remaining 2 graham cracker halves, forming a sandwich.

Substitution Tip: Try swiping a little peanut butter or jam on the top graham cracker halves before smashing them down, or try white or dark chocolate.

PER SERVING: Calories: 198; Total fat: 8g; Carbohydrates: 30g; Fiber: 1g; Protein: 3g

Mug Birthday Cake

MICROWAVE

ONE BOWL

VEGETARIAN

Serves 1

PREP TIME
10 minutes

COOK TIME
3 minutes, plus cooling

Birthdays demand cake. And just because you don't have an oven—and your RA will flip out if you light a candle in your dorm—doesn't mean you're out of luck. This microwave cake whips up in minutes (making it also perfect for when you learn at 8 p.m. that it was your suitemate's big day), and it's every bit as delicious as anything you'd buy at a store.

FOR THE CAKE

2 tablespoons unsalted butter
⅓ cup all-purpose flour
2 tablespoons sugar
¼ teaspoon baking powder
⅛ teaspoon salt
1½ tablespoons water
1 teaspoon vanilla extract
1 teaspoon rainbow sprinkles, plus more for decorating
1 tablespoon frosting (page 135)

FOR THE FROSTING

1 tablespoon unsalted butter
½ cup powdered sugar
¼ teaspoon vanilla extract
1 to 2 teaspoons milk
1 or more drops food coloring of choice

TO MAKE THE CAKE

1. Place the butter in a large microwave-safe bowl and microwave for 20 to 25 seconds, or until melted.
2. Add the flour, sugar, baking powder, and salt and stir until combined.
3. Stir in the water and vanilla.

4. Fold in the rainbow sprinkles without really stirring them in (mixing too much will cause the colors to run).
5. Microwave for 45 to 55 seconds. The cake will be very pale, but it should be springy to the touch when you gently press your finger on top. Or insert a toothpick into the center of the cake and if it comes back clean, the cake is done. If the cake is runny in the center, reduce the power to 80 percent and cook in 20-second intervals until baked.
6. Let cool before frosting.

TO MAKE THE FROSTING

1. To make the frosting, place the butter in a small microwave-safe bowl and microwave in 15-second intervals until melted.
2. Add the powdered sugar, vanilla, and 1 teaspoon of milk. Stir until smooth. Gradually stir in the remaining 1 teaspoon of milk, if needed, until the mixture is a spreadable consistency. Add the food coloring, stirring until completely combined. Add more food coloring, a drop at a time, until you achieve the shade you like.

MAKE IT VEGAN: For the cake, use melted coconut oil instead of butter in a 1:1 swap. For the frosting, use a nut milk instead of cow's milk and swap the butter for melted coconut oil in a 1:1 swap.

PER SERVING: (CAKE) Calories: 554; Total fat: 27g; Carbohydrates: 72g; Fiber: 1g; Protein: 5g

---

PER SERVING: (FROSTING) Calories: 341; Total fat: 12g; Carbohydrates: 60g; Fiber: 0g; Protein: 0g

Deep-Dish Microwave Cookie

MICROWAVE

15 MINUTES OR LESS

VEGETARIAN

Serves 2

PREP TIME
5 minutes

COOK TIME
1 minute

Substitution Tip: If you don't have Greek yogurt on hand, use an egg yolk instead. If you don't have brown sugar, granulated sugar works, too. The cookie will have a lighter color and texture and it won't have the same caramelized flavor but will taste yummy.

You know those deep-dish skillet cookies often served at chain restaurants with a scoop of ice cream on top? The ones with the crisp edges and chewy, gooey center? Yeah, you do. With this recipe, you can get that flavor right at home and your life will never be the same.

1 tablespoon unsalted butter
2 tablespoons light brown sugar
⅛ teaspoon vanilla extract
1 tablespoon vanilla Greek yogurt
¼ cup all-purpose flour
¼ teaspoon baking powder
⅛ teaspoon salt
2 tablespoons semisweet chocolate chips

1. Place the butter in a large microwave-safe bowl and microwave for 20 to 25 seconds, or until melted.
2. Add the brown sugar, vanilla, and yogurt, and stir to combine.
3. Add the flour, baking powder, and salt, and stir to combine. Fold in the chocolate chips until evenly mixed.
4. Microwave for 40 to 45 seconds. Let the cookie rest 10 to 15 seconds, before using a toothpick to check the center. If it's covered in raw batter, microwave for 10 to 15 seconds more. If the toothpick is clean or has just a few crumbs, the cookie is ready to enjoy.

PER SERVING: Calories: 218; Total fat: 10g; Carbohydrates: 30g; Fiber: 2g; Protein: 4g

Apple Crisp for One

Get the flavors of apple pie without having to roll out piecrust. The cinnamon-y streusel really makes the crisp, so don't skimp on it. In fact, you may want to triple the recipe and keep it on hand in the freezer because, after trying it once, you'll want to have this apple crisp again and again.

MICROWAVE

15 MINUTES OR LESS

VEGETARIAN

Serves 1

PREP TIME
10 minutes

COOK TIME
2½ minutes

FOR THE STREUSEL

1 teaspoon all-purpose flour

1½ teaspoons sugar

⅛ teaspoon ground cinnamon

1 tablespoon cold unsalted butter, diced

Ice cream, for serving (optional)

FOR THE APPLE FILLING

1 Granny Smith apple, peeled, cored, and diced

1 teaspoon all-purpose flour

1 teaspoon sugar

½ teaspoon freshly squeezed lemon juice

¼ teaspoon ground cinnamon

Preparation Tip: To feed a crowd, multiply this recipe by 5 and bake in a 2-quart casserole dish in a conventional oven at 350°F for 30 to 35 minutes, or until the apples are tender.

TO MAKE THE STREUSEL

1. In a small bowl, stir together the flour, sugar, and cinnamon.
2. Add the butter and, using a fork, mix it in, breaking up the mixture to form small crumbles. Set aside.

CONTINUED

Apple Crisp for One CONTINUED

TO MAKE THE APPLE FILLING

1. In a microwave-safe mug, stir together the apple, flour, sugar, lemon juice, and cinnamon.
2. Sprinkle the streusel in an even layer on top of the apple mixture.

TO MAKE THE CRISP

Microwave the crisp for 2 to 2½ minutes, or until the apples are tender. Serve with a scoop of ice cream (if using).

PER SERVING: Calories: 262; Total fat: 12g; Carbohydrates: 38g; Fiber: 5g; Protein: 2g

Cheesecake Truffles

Sometimes you just want cheesecake. But dealing with water baths and springform pans can be a total hassle, especially when you're cooking in a kitchenette. These shortcut truffles solve that problem. You can enjoy the flavor you crave in minutes, without having to invest in a ton of baking gear. They also make a pretty great last-minute birthday gift.

MICROWAVE

5-INGREDIENT

VEGETARIAN

Serves 4

PREP TIME
10 minutes, plus 10 minutes freezing

COOK TIME
1½ minutes

½ (8-ounce) package cream cheese, at room temperature

1½ teaspoons sugar

15 vanilla wafer cookies

¾ cup semisweet chocolate chips

1 tablespoon vegetable oil

1. Line a plate with plastic wrap.
2. In a large bowl, stir together the cream cheese and sugar. (For best results, use an electric hand mixer.)
3. Place the cookies in a resealable plastic bag. Seal the bag and use a large, heavy spoon or textbook to smash the cookies into fine crumbs. Set aside 2 tablespoons of crumbs. Pour the rest of the crumbs into the cream cheese mixture and stir to combine.
4. Roll the mixture into 1-inch balls and place them on the prepared plate in a single layer. Place the plate in the freezer while you prepare the chocolate. (If you don't have a freezer, the fridge is fine.)

Preparation Tip: As you're working with the chocolate and it starts to cool, it will thicken. The consistency should be a little thicker than paint. If the chocolate starts getting gloppy, microwave it for 20 seconds and give it a stir. Still too thick? Try adding a ¼ teaspoon more oil.

CONTINUED

Cheesecake Truffles CONTINUED

5. In a small microwave-safe bowl, stir together the chocolate chips and vegetable oil. Microwave for 30 seconds, stir, and microwave in 20-second intervals, stirring between each, until the chocolate is completely melted.
6. Using a fork, lower each cheesecake ball into the chocolate mixture. Use a spoon to cover the ball with chocolate and slowly lift out of the bowl, shaking off any excess chocolate. Place the ball back on the plate and sprinkle with the reserved cookie bits. Repeat with the remaining cheesecake balls. Place the balls in the freezer or refrigerator for at least 10 minutes until the chocolate sets.

PER SERVING: (3 TRUFFLES) Calories: 399; Total fat: 27g; Carbohydrates: 39g; Fiber: 3g; Protein: 5g

Measurement Conversions

Volume Equivalents (Liquid)

U.S. STANDARD	U.S. STANDARD (OUNCES)	METRIC (APPROXIMATE)
2 tablespoons	1 fl. oz.	30 mL
¼ cup	2 fl. oz.	60 mL
½ cup	4 fl. oz.	120 mL
1 cup	8 fl. oz.	240 mL
1½ cups	12 fl. oz.	355 mL
2 cups or 1 pint	16 fl. oz.	475 mL
4 cups or 1 quart	32 fl. oz.	1 L
1 gallon	128 fl. oz.	4 L

Oven Temperatures

FAHRENHEIT	CELSIUS (APPROXIMATE)
250°F	120°C
300°F	150°C
325°F	165°C
350°F	180°C
375°F	190°C
400°F	200°C
425°F	220°C
450°F	230°C

Weight Equivalents

U.S. STANDARD	METRIC (APPROXIMATE)
½ ounce	15 g
1 ounce	30 g
2 ounces	60 g
4 ounces	115 g
8 ounces	225 g
12 ounces	340 g
16 ounces or 1 pound	455 g

Volume Equivalents (Dry)

U.S. STANDARD	METRIC (APPROXIMATE)
⅛ teaspoon	0.5 mL
¼ teaspoon	1 mL
½ teaspoon	2 mL
¾ teaspoon	4 mL
1 teaspoon	5 mL
1 tablespoon	15 mL
¼ cup	59 mL
⅓ cup	79 mL
½ cup	118 mL
⅔ cup	156 mL
¾ cup	177 mL
1 cup	235 mL
2 cups or 1 pint	475 mL
3 cups	700 mL
4 cups or 1 quart	1 L

Resources

"Basically." *Bon Appétit*, 2018. www.bonappetit.com/basically.

Davison, Candace. "Collegiate Cook Recipes." Collegiate Cook, 2010. www.collegiatecook.com/.

"Delish." Delish.com, 2015. www.delish.com/.

"Her Campus." Her Campus, 2009. www.hercampus.com/.

Joachim, David. *A Man, A Can, A Plan: 50 Great Guy Meals Even You Can Make*. Emmaus, PA: Rodale Books, 2002.

Moncel, Beth. "Delicious Recipes Designed for Small Budgets." *Budget Bytes*, 2010. www.budgetbytes.com/.

Okamoto, Toni. *Plant-Based on a Budget: Delicious Vegan Recipes for Under $30 a Week, in Less than 30 Minutes a Meal*. Dallas: BenBella Books, 2019.

Rhee, Chungah. "Damn Delicious." *Damn Delicious*, 2011. https://damndelicious.net.

Robinson, Claire. *5 Ingredient Fix: Easy, Elegant, and Irresistible Recipes*. New York: Grand Central Life & Style, 2010.

Saltz, Joanna, and the Editors of Delish. *Delish: Eat Like Every Day's the Weekend*. New York: Houghton Mifflin Harcourt, 2018.

Teigen, Chrissy, and Adeena Sussman. *Cravings: Hungry for More*. New York: Clarkson Potter, 2018.

References

Chapter Three

Petruzzello, Melissa. "Why Does Cilantro Taste Like Soap to Some People?" *Encyclopædia Britannica.* Accessed June 25, 2019. www.britannica.com/story/why-does-cilantro-taste-like-soap-to-some-people.

Chapter Four

Grech, Dan, and Scott Finn. "The Cuban Sandwich Crisis: Tampa v. Miami for the Win." NPR. April 21, 2012. Accessed June 30, 2019. www.npr.org/sections/thesalt/2012/04/21/151050107/the-cuban-sandwich-crisis-tampa-v-miami-for-the-win.

Chapter Six

Stradley, Linda. "Perfect Poached Eggs." *What's Cooking America.* September 1, 2017. Accessed July 1, 2019. https://whatscookingamerica.net/Eggs/PoachEgg.htm.

Chapter Eight

Tamanna, Nahid, and Niaz Mahmood. "Food Processing and Maillard Reaction Products: Effect on Human Health and Nutrition." *International Journal of Food Science* 2015 (January 8, 2015): 1–6. Accessed July 1, 2019. http://dx.doi:10.1155/2015/526762.

Index

C

D

E

F

G

M

Q

R

S

T

V

Acknowledgments

Finally, my overzealous appetite pays off! This book wouldn't be possible without my roommates and friends who willingly sampled my dorm room dishes (and disasters)—Ashleigh, Lyndsey, Brenna, Sean, Matt, Erin, Chris, Cynthia, Victoria: THANK YOU. There was a lot of trial and error in those early days—particularly during that phase when I made dishes with a clothing iron, because, well, dorm appliance options are limited.

Thank you, also, to those who encouraged me to blog about my experiments, an activity that landed me a job at Delish—and helped me gain the attention of this very publisher. The Callisto Media team has been amazing to work with every step of the way. Crystal, thank you for your thoughtful feedback!

Most of all, thanks to Nathan and Emerie, who watched me test (and retest) and who sampled roughly 75 dishes in a six-week period for the making of this cookbook. You guys are the best of the best.

And to my parents, and siblings—Tyler, Kirsten, and Carson: You've championed every scheme I've had over the years and for that I'm beyond grateful. XO.

About the Author

Candace Braun Davison has been writing about food since 2009, when she launched Collegiate-Cook.com, a site that focuses on recipes and cooking shortcuts for students. When she isn't trying to hack microwave meals, she works for *House Beautiful* magazine and lives in New York with her husband, Nate, and daughter, Emerie. Oh, and she's perpetually searching for the world's best chocolate chip cookie. So, if you find it, let her know, okay?

CPSIA information can be obtained
at www.ICGtesting.com
Printed in the USA
LVHW071403040922
727590LV00019B/1332

9 781641 529389